THE
WORDS
WE
USE

To my son, Christopher

THE

WORDS

WE

USE

by

Robert

Lord

KAHN & AVERILL
LONDON

First published in 1994 by
Kahn & Averill
9 Harrington Road, London SW7 3ES

Copyright © 1994 by Robert Lord

British Library Cataloguing in Publication Data

A catalogue record for this book is available from the British Library

ISBN 1 871082 44 7

Printed in Great Britain by
Redwood Books, Trowbridge, Wilts

CONTENTS

Foreword

1. What is a word?   1

2. The trouble with dictionaries   8

3. The use of words: what happens when we talk   16

4. How did words originate?   22

5. How do words change their meaning?   28

6. Word borrowing   40

7. How are new words created?   50

8. Words as structures   57

9. How do we learn to use words?   66

10. Choosing between words – words in context   76

11. On the tip of one's tongue   83

12. The written word   90

13. Words and the poet   99

14. Sticks and stones: words as reality   108

15. Afterword   115

FOREWORD

This book is an attempt to introduce the reader to some of the main facets of words, as these make their presence felt in our own day. The intention is not to be exhaustive, but to stimulate. Nor have we a textbook here, or a substitute for one. Nevertheless, the reader who persists for all fifteen chapters should have the feeling that much ground has been covered; sufficient at any rate to reveal that the word, under the scrutiny of various modern analytical approaches, has not proved any more tractable than it was in the time of Aristotle or Francis Bacon. The more we come to know about words, the less final our judgments. The twentieth century has produced an explosion in knowledge and awareness and, correspondingly, the word has expanded to fill the whole universe so far created by this explosion. Everywhere we look, we find our own reflection in this human artefact that, like Eve from Adam, has its starting point in our own being, in ways we never quite manage to fathom, in hidden ways, the answer always lying just beyond our reach. For those readers with time and inclination to pursue particular lines of approach, short sections of Notes and Suggested Further Reading at the end of each chapter have been included.

I am deeply in debt to those who have read my various drafts and provided encouragement, especially Terry Gordon who went through in meticulous detail sections of a much longer work of similar coverage but, as yet, unpublished. For any errors or lapses remaining, however, no one but myself is responsible. And, needless to say, I am grateful for the impetus provided by the many scholars either explicitly mentioned, or implicitly somehow present, a few omnipresent, in these pages. I also want to thank Anita Fung Ka Wai, Ada Lee Sin Kwan and Ophelia Wong Lai Fong who have shown such patience in the various stages of word processing. Without them, this book would have been long delayed.

THE
WORDS
WE
USE

1

WHAT IS A WORD?

Have you ever wondered, especially when you are searching for the right word for a particular occasion, what is a word? What are those things hanging on the tip of the tongue?

Well, when we look at them closely they seem to be just groups of letters, spoken or spelled. We know that sometimes they are more than just that, but we don't seem to have the necessary conceptual equipment to handle them more meaningfully.

The easiest thing is perhaps to be simple-minded, and say that, whatever else it might be, a word is a series of letters bounded by spaces, or a series of sounds marked by pauses, and leave it at that. Trivial though such an approach would be, it does contain some deep element of truth, of which all the resources of modern linguistic science can do no more than skirt the edges.

One of the difficulties with this 'word boundary' type of approach is that it can be self-fulling and circular. Our words in the particular language or languages we speak are as they are because that is how we feel them to be. Notice, the verb 'feel' is deliberately used, rather than 'perceive' or 'conceive', or anything else. We *feel*, for instance, that *blackbird* when it stands for a species of bird is one word, whereas when it simply denotes any 'black' 'bird', like a raven or crow, we are dealing with two words, not one. In the latter instance a printed space is used between the two 'words'. More subtly, in speech, there is a shift of stress: *'blackbird* ('species') becomes *black 'bird* ('any black bird') by shifting its stress. In other cases, we 'feel' differently. Most English speakers would say that *red wine* is two words, whether it means a generic type of wine which can be anything between purple and deep red, or whether it means a wine of red colour, contrasted with 'white' or 'rosé'. Yet, perversely it might seem, *hotbed* is 'felt' to be a single word, regardless of whether it means 'a bed of earth heated by manure' or 'a place that favours the rapid spread of some condition, like vice or corruption'. In neither case is there any change, such as a shift of stress or word boundary: *red wine* is *red wine* in all situations, and *hotbed* is *hotbed*.

As a matter of fact, speakers of different languages have different ideas about what constitutes a word. Speakers of Chinese are convinced that words are one syllable in length — all words of more than one syllable are simply compounds — and as if to prove it they write each syllable with one discrete written character. Yet in everyday speech their words, as defined by other sometimes more scientific criteria, are usually of two syllables or more in length. Nevertheless, because the Chinese speaker 'feels' each word is one syllable in length only, he prefers to think of words of more than one syllable as 'compound' words; just as, perhaps, in English we think of *disc jockey* as a compound word, for the reason that *disc* and *jockey* have an independent existence of their own. When we take a look at a range of other languages, our whole confidence seems to be undermined: after all, in English, words do begin with recognisable sounds or letters — A for *apple*, B for *bun*, C for *cat*, etc. The 'a' of *apple* is always 'a', and 'b' in *bun* always 'b', and so on. But in Celtic and several other groups of languages, this integrity appears somehow absent. If, for example, I try looking up the Welsh word-form *fasged* in a Welsh dictionary, I will not find it. Because, first, I need to know that in a (seemingly bewildering) range of ordinary instances the first letter of the root word *basged* — which is in the dictionary and means 'basket' — has changed from *b* to *f*. Similarly, if I look up the form *ngheffyl* I will get nowhere, unless I am aware that this is what becomes of 'root' word *ceffyl* 'horse' in particular contexts. All this, it goes without saying, is the most natural thing in the world for a native speaker of Welsh. It is only a puzzle to the foreign learner.

As we move to more exotic languages and away from the centres of civilisation, we come across the most extraordinary 'words'. Here is an example of a whole (i.e. not a compound) word from a North American Indian language, Paiute. The word is *wii-to-kuchum-punku-rügani-yugwi-va-ntü-m(ü)* 'knife - black - buffalo - pet - cut up - sit - (future) - (participle) - (animate plural)', and to render it in English we have to use something approaching an entire sentence: 'They who are going to sit and cut up with a knife a black cow or bull.'

After this little round of culture shock, therefore, let us return to the safety and comfort of English; and ask ourselves again, in the context of a familiar language: What is a word?

Let us begin, at random, with an everyday word like *head*.

We all know the basic meaning of *head*. We may become growingly surprised, even a little alarmed, as we read through the listing of less common meanings, like 'head of hair', 'head of cattle', 'the rounded or compact part of a plant', 'summit', 'head of water', 'head of a page', 'issue' and so on. Did you know for instance that *head* also means 'the antlers of a deer', 'pressure of a confined body of vapour', 'the commencement of a zodiacal sign', 'the thick end of a chisel or wedge' , 'a bundle of flax', 'a tile used at the eaves of a roof' and 'a rammer for crushing quartz'? You failed to recognise all these 'specialist' meanings?... I wonder just how many readers knew them all. The point being made is that there are many everyday words in any language, the specialised meanings of which we are not expected to know, unless we happen to be familiar with that particular field of activity. If I am a builder, I will know the meaning *head* = 'tile', or if I am an astrologer I would know that *head* is the commencement of a zodiacal sign.

Now let us turn to two different kinds of simple word: the personal pronouns *I* and *you*. We use these words all the time and yet usually do not recognise that they are among the most puzzling words in English, or indeed in any language. In all languages, the pronouns *I* and *you* change places very often,

3

sometimes more than once in a single interaction between two speakers:

Did you like her new hair do?
No, I did not. What about you?
Well, I'm not too sure myself. Didn't you think it rather affected?
You're dead right — affected it certainly was ...

Whenever I refer to myself as 'I' in the course of the most ordinary of conversations, I am referring not to a physiologically ordered mass of molecules — in this case my own body — or even an ego, but to a verbal role performed in the actual situation there and then. Every single time 'I' refer to myself, using the pronouns *I* or *me*, I am making a *new* reference to a *new* (however slightly modified) referent. As Roland Barthes put it: 'The *I* of the one who writes *I* is not the same as the *I* which is read by *thou*'. No matter who I am; whenever I speak, it is not just a question of a simple 'I' addressing another speaker, but the 'I' experiencing the presence of others within oneself. Put in another way, 'I' signifies neither me nor anyone else; but only 'the person uttering the present instance of discourse containing 'I'.

Just in case you are beginning to feel a little uneasy, not only with this dose of discourse metaphysics but also with your degree of familiarity with your own language, or at least (in the case of speakers of English as a second language) with a language you know very well, you can hopefully reassure yourself as to the stock of words you can actually recognise and use by turning to a good English dictionary.

Or can you?

Look out *The Shorter Oxford English Dictionary* (3rd Edn.), and turn up page 943, headed *hyperaemia — hypertrophy*. How many words did you recognise? How many could you have given even approximate meanings to? If your score is higher than fifty per cent, you are doing remarkably well indeed. Don't despair though if you only got 20 per cent or even less, you are still doing pretty well.

This is part of the trouble with a language like English. It is full of word borrowings — on that particular page all from Greek, or at any rate adaptations of Greek; almost as if English has become

4

a 'word-bin', a receptacle for just about every word that anybody has ever needed and incidentally committed to writing. *The Shorter Oxford Dictionary* records only words deemed to be standard. It does not generally record dialectisms. For these you have to turn to a dialect dictionary. Nor does it generally record regionalisms. If you want to know about English usage in Jamaica, for instance, you would consult, say, a dictionary of Jamaican English.

Quite often we become so familiar and feel so comfortable with the words we use that we don't stop to think about them. They are like domesticated animals and we take them for granted.

From this point in our survey we could strike out in any of a whole range of directions, but let us explore, just a little way at least, a few of these 'domesticated' words.

The word *laser* is familiar to every schoolboy, even more perhaps than to his parents. He is the one more likely to be able to come up with the information that *laser* is simply the acronym of '*L*ight *A*mplification by the *S*timulated *E*mission of *R*adiation'. *Laser* is an everyday word, and yet to comprehend the real meaning of the word we would need to possess an advanced knowledge of physics.

The word *laser* has been chosen as an example for its obviousness. You might well react by objecting that, in the case of words like *laser*, we do not really need to know its meaning as defined by the physicist, any more than we need to be any better informed than the layman of equally well domesticated entities like *electricity* or *television* or *semi-conductor* or *chromosome*. If I had chosen a much more humdrum word, like *apple* or *teacup*, no one would have noticed that there could be a problem. Yet, an ordinary *apple* raises just as many questions as the most abstruse physics. We talk about 'apples' as if there were nothing remarkable about them, unless we happen to be a biochemist, a fruit connoisseur, a painter like Cézanne, or an expert apple-grower. In fact, when you think about it, when we talk about an apple we are virtually never saying anything worthwhile or essential about apples. We buy, cook and eat apples, even grow them, without bothering to consider what really is an apple.

But again, you will have the very reasonable reaction that if we took time over such considerations we would never get beyond a single sentence a day, or a week even, and our communicative competence would be reduced to vanishing point.

I have gone by such a circuitous route in order to get to the heart of the matter. What are words really?

A short and superficial answer to such a question — because actually no one really knows what words are — is that they are no mere series of letters bounded by spaces, nor for that matter series of sounds separated by pauses, any more than my favourite jacket is a facsimile of my untidy self. The frayed pockets, torn linings, and sleeves shiny at the elbow may tell you something that could be inferred about my habits and even my character, but it will not tell you much, if anything, about the essential me.

The only marked resemblance between a word and my battered but beloved jacket is that it is not something made or even contributed to by me. It is something I pick up from others, learn to use, and can easily discard when I have no further need for it. While I use it, or hear or read it, I seldom stop to consider what this humble word is.

Let me then try out on you a tentative definition; and allow me thus to propose that a word is, whatever else it might be, at least two things: (1) a piece of feeling, and (2) a piece of culture.

Before going on to discuss these two notions, it should be noted that I have not said anything more about letters, or sounds, or spaces. Perhaps even more surprisingly, I have not said anything about concepts, or ideas.

I have deliberately bypassed the latter because the whole activity of mental representation, for all that it is vital in itself, is implicit in feelings and in culture. Let one thing be made clear, however: the feeling that I am referring to has nothing directly to do with adrenalin levels or the physical emotional response of the body (though it has to be insisted that feeling does not amount to much unless the state of the body is somehow affected by what is felt). The ability of naive American Indian speakers to identify the words of their own languages by intuition is something that impressed the linguist and anthropologist Edward Sapir very greatly. This was a feeling, worth more than any amount of purely theoretical analysis, an aesthetic sense, which convinced Sapir of 'the definite plastic unity of the word'.

As for culture, this of course has nothing to do with attending symphony concerts or visiting art exhibitions. By culture is meant those discrete elements of our lives that are shared by others, and responded to in a similar manner by others. A cultural item thus may be anything from an exquisite fragment of the Elgin Marbles to an ordinary rain shower, a beech tree in first leaf, a picnic, or an evening at the pub. All cultural items are artefacts in that they have been somehow fashioned, even created, by human beings like ourselves. There was no 'magic' in the modern non-witchcraft sense ('There's magic in her voice') until Shakespeare made it. Nor was there any law of 'gravity' until Newton established it. Even the rocks and trees and streams — things we have ostensibly no control over whatsoever — were shaped as felt things and parts of our cultural lives by countless generations of predecessors, all except the most recent of them preliterate, but endowing the world around them with so much sense as their words would allow them.

Notes and suggested Further Reading

It is not easy to find anything lengthy and substantial in English on the nature of words. This is, at least in part, because modern linguists have on the whole fought shy of attempts to really come to grips with the word. Modern linguistics has been more comfortable with concepts like morpheme, lexeme, moneme, semanteme, and the like. However, excellent chapters are to be found in Stephen Ullmann's Semantics: An Introduction to the Study of Meaning *(especially Chapters 2 & 3) (London, 1962). Readers might also find interesting the paper by M.A.K. Halliday ('Lexis as a linguistic level') in C.E. Bazell et al (eds):* In Memory of J.R. Firth *(London, 1966). Edward Sapir's short book* Language *(2nd Edn., London, 1949), although vintage, still provides a useful introduction to the study of language. In particular he discusses the aesthetic nature of the word. For the discussion on the use of 'I', see a short essay by Roland Barthes, entitled 'To write: Intransitive Verb?' in R. Macksey and E. Donato (eds):* The Structuralist Controversy: The Language of Criticism and the Sciences of Man *(Baltimore, 1972)*

2

THE TROUBLE WITH DICTIONARIES

We are all more or less familiar with dictionaries, and some of us would feel lost without them. As one writer has put it,

> 'Dictionaries, like electric lights and written constitutions, must be ranked among the basic facts of modern civilised life. Without them, our western culture would no doubt survive, but only at the price of a notable increase in frustration, confusion and unhappiness.'

Dictionaries can be daunting — there seem to be so many words we don't know the meaning of! — and yet they are reassuring too: if we do come across a word we would like to know the meaning of, we can nearly always find it in some dictionary or other.

A dictionary, or lexicon, is an informative alphabetical listing of words used in a language. Generally speaking, the larger the dictionary, the more words there will be. The increase in size is only partly accounted for by an increase in information, but partly also by the admission of rare, highly specialised, or archaic words. There are, it goes without saying, many kinds of dictionaries. The dictionaries familiar to us in English are alphabetic dictionaries, like *Webster's Third New International Dictionary* or *The Shorter Oxford English Dictionary*, for example. That means that all the items included in the dictionary are listed in alphabetical order. English dictionaries follow the Roman, Greek the Greek, and Russian the Russian alphabetical order. In languages which don't have an alphabet, like Chinese or Japanese, stroke order is used, each written 'character' having a unique arrangement and number of brush strokes.

Not all dictionaries are alphabetic. *Roget's Thesaurus*, for example, does not follow an alphabetical, but a conceptual order. Only the index is alphabetical. Further, not all alphabetic dictionaries are lexical. Some traditions have made greater use of the encyclopaedic dictionary, one of the more prominent examples being the French *Encyclopédie Larousse*. But in this chapter we will be dealing only with alphabetical, lexical dictionaries.

Of the many types of alphabetical lexical dictionary, furthermore, we shall be concerning ourselves only with 'monolingual' dictionaries. We shall be leaving aside any consideration of 'bilingual' dictionaries, as well as specialist, dialect, rhyming, reversing dictionaries, or indeed any other kind of lexicon.

It is curious to note that the earliest monolingual dictionary in English was published only towards the end of Shakespeare's lifetime. Cawdrey's *Table Alphabeticall* of 1604, however, would not stand comparison with its contemporary Italian Dictionary *Vocabolario degli Accademici della Crusca* (1612). But, at least, it was the harbinger of a long series of dictionaries, reaching a level of maturity only in the middle of the eighteenth century, in Scott-Bailey's *New Universal Etymological English Dictionary* and especially in Dr. Johnson's more famous *Dictionary of the English Language*.

Though dictionaries have been a blessing ever since that time, this blessing has been a mixed one. The dictionary has proved the greatest impediment of all in the way of any move towards a breakaway from a tendency to regard dictionary entries as hard facts, indisputable and given for all time, as if inscribed on tablets of stone.

Part of the problem is that the dictionary-makers — the

9

'lexicographers' — for all the distinguished exponents in their ranks (Dr. Johnson was merely among the first of a long line), have not really understood what they were doing. This was not their fault, however, since a plausibly scientific understanding of the nature of vocabulary and how vocabulary fits into the whole picture of language is scarcely more than half a century old. Virtually all of the great dictionary-makers were dead before this scientific enterprise dawned.

Much more serious is the fact that the present-day lexicographer is generally barely aware of the changes that have taken place in our theoretical understanding of the lexicon. And, worse still, even prominent linguistic theorists have neglected the lexicon altogether, and tended to treat it as a mere appendage of language; when, in actual fact, as every man-in-the-street knows, the words we use and the way we use them are the most important — for some the only really important — ingredients of the languages we speak and write.

Let us, then, take a look at what a typical dictionary actually contains.

The monolingual dictionary most familiar to us is in essence a list of lexical entries. Each entry is prefaced by a 'head-word', presented in standard spelling (orthography), and arranged in alphabetical order relative to other head-words. Dictionaries vary quite a bit in the kind of information provided in the entries. These entries themselves may range from simple glosses of the type: APPLE = 'a kind of fruit', to the fuller description provided by such dictionaries as the Shorter Oxford ('The round firm fleshy fruit of a Rosaceous tree ... found widely ... in Europe, etc., and cultivated in innumerable varieties all over the two Temperate Zones'). Dictionaries providing richer descriptions of this sort will probably also contain information on pronunciation, etymology, as well as illustrative quotations.

Probably most people, if challenged, would claim that what a dictionary does is to give the meanings of words, with some indications about their use. But, strange as it may seem, dictionaries do not provide us with the 'meanings' of words at all. Indeed, some authorities would deny that there are such things as word meanings. Dictionaries provide only 'glosses', ways of paraphras-

10

ing a word by another group of words. Or, as the British philosopher J. L. Austin put it: all the dictionary can do is, whenever we look up the meaning of a word, to suggest aids to the understanding of sentences in which it occurs. What has 'meaning', if we follow this line of approach, is not the individual word, but the sentence in which it occurs. We are informed by the dictionary, for instance, that APPLE is a noun, that it is generically a fruit, and so forth; to the extent that we can know in advance when 'apple' would be the appropriate choice in a particular sentence (as if we didn't know already!). We know that 'apple' would be the wrong choice in any of the following:

(1) *An* _____ *is a type of cheese*
(2) *He* _____ *half a mile before coming to a halt.*
(3) *When he arrived home the* _____ *he had just bought had turned into a soggy mass at the bottom of his briefcase.*

Sentence (1) must be impossible, because the dictionary, if not our own intuition, tells us that an apple is a fruit. Sentence (2) is equally impossible because the space after 'he' requires a verb; and 'apple', we are told, is a noun. Example (3) may be just possible in real life, but the dictionary specifies firmness; not the soft kind of fruit, like raspberries, which can easily turn to pulp.

If we consider the matter more closely, we will see that dictionaries make use of a variety of different kinds of 'gloss'. Sometimes entries are glossed by means of *synonyms*. The entry STIFF = 'rigid; tight; inflexible of purpose' would be of this kind, but this type of gloss would not occur so frequently in the larger standard dictionaries.

Another highly valued type of gloss is denotation. Denotation relies on definition of the type illustrated above by APPLE. Alternatively, it may depend on ostensive definition, which meets empirical criteria to the extent of providing sample 'denotata', or concrete instances, or both. *The Shorter Oxford English Dictionary*, for example, combines denotative and ostensive definition for one of the separate 'meanings' of the entry VEHICLE: 'A means of conveyance provided with wheels or runners and used for the carriage of persons or goods; a carriage, cart, waggon, sledge, etc.'

Still another type of gloss, sometimes found in dictionaries, is one in which the term is exhibited in actual use. Thus, DIAGO-NAL might be defined by the sentence: 'A square has two diagonals, and each of them divides the square into two right-angled isosceles triangles.' The latter type of dictionary defini-tion, which we may call *operational* or *contextual*, though it may be just right for DIAGONAL, would be less than ideal, say, for an entry like CAT, whose contextual range of meaning could never be exhausted, however much we might multiply instances of the following kind: *'The _____ is a mouse-catching animal'*. *'I bought some fish for my _____'*. *'Our _____ is black and little'*. *'This _____ is a Siamese'*, and so forth.

So far, none of the procedures for dealing with word meanings gets us anywhere near what we feel to be the word's *intrinsic* meaning; even less do we catch its quality, flavour or particular weight, its intractability — something familiar to every writer.

Take for instance *denotation*, which seems to get us closest to that elusive meaning we are looking for. APPLE we learnt *denotes*: 'the round firm fleshy fruit of a Rosaceous tree, etc.' That seems to fill in a great part of our quest, until we start thinking about it. To begin with, we must put out of our minds any possibility that 'denote' means anything like 'refer'. Individual common nouns, the philosophers have convinced us, cannot refer; only complete statements of certain types (e.g. *This fruit is an apple*, or *Would you like this apple?*, etc.) can refer. Denotation is more like the ghost of reference. To take a further example, in the sentence *This is a picture of a dinosaur*, neither *picture* nor *dinosaur* refer to anything in particular. It is only the sentence as a whole, in actual use, that refers, and enables us to identify the separate 'referents' *picture* and *dinosaur*. The dinosaur, we learn from the sentence, is not a *real* dinosaur but some representation of a dinosaur. The picture is probably not the kind that is hung in a gallery, but more likely — though the sentence doesn't tell us for sure — is probably an illustration in a book or magazine.

If we persist in trying to find out what denotation can possibly be, we are likely to end up with an unhelpfully abstruse statement to the effect that denotation is a relationship which holds between a word and certain 'denotata'. These denotata can be and are quite often persons, things, places, properties, processes and activities which are external to language. But denotata are seldom easy to pin down or set limits to. With words like *rhinoceros* or *pterodactyl* there is no serious problem but, with the mass of our everyday words, difficulties seem never-ending. The denotata given for apple in the Shorter Oxford may seem all very well until we run into *toffee apples*, expressions like *apple of my eye*, the brand name for a personal computer, and a host of other wayward 'meanings'. What is the way out of this problem? Should we simply list all the dictionary meanings, identify these as the denotata of 'apple', and leave it at that? Not a very satisfactory way of understanding word meaning, you might well feel. But if you are happy with that sort of solution, try it with the words DO or GO. The latter word occupies, despite rigorous lexicographical economy, no less than six columns in *The Shorter Oxford English Dictionary*.

That is not the end of our quandary. Before we reach the conclusion that our inventory of denotata is complete, someone sooner or later is bound to use a word in a wilfully deviant way.

Take the dictionary entry TABLE, for example. The dictionary provides us with the assurance that a mathematical or statistical table, or a timetable, belong to different denotational classes from those 'articles of furniture consisting of a flat top of wood, etc.' But then some eccentric friend invites me to supper. Noticing my surprise at seeing nothing resembling a table in his place, he tries to reassure me by pointing to the floor, saying 'This is my table, O.K.?' Such deviant 'metaphorical' uses of words do nothing to lend solid value to the concept of denotation. After all, many meanings listed in the dictionary originally had a metaphorical meaning too, and quite a few still have. It seems that there must be far more to denotation, and word meaning in general, than meets the eye.

As soon as we start thinking fundamentally about dictionaries we find ourselves in a hall of mirrors. Dictionary entries, we end up by concluding, provide not the 'meanings' of words, but only glosses, alternative paraphrases and equivalents. Dictionaries do not lead us into the real world in any reliable way. As we have just seen, the dictionary account of TABLE, mentioned above, will do very well until it is used deviantly (according to the dictionary) but still comprehensibly.

Dictionaries, as a matter of fact, have to be constantly revised to take account of such deviations. Once these deviations become widely accepted a new denotative category has to be set up. Such has happened, in recent memory, with words like *gay*, *square*, *beat*, *rock* and many others.

Obviously, there must be some correspondence between what dictionaries tell us and the way people recognise and use words in real life. But it is not correct to say that the relationship is in any way parallel, or one-to-one: we cannot say that the lexical competence of the ordinary speaker is in the form presented by the dictionary, as some modern linguists would have us believe. A few moments reflection is sufficient to convince anyone that we do not, as a general rule, either use or interpret words in accordance with their dictionary definitions. More usually, we are taken aback at the discrepancy between the way we use a particular word and, when we consult it, the dictionary's opinion about its use.

This is not to say, however, that dictionaries do not have their uses. Dictionaries, it cannot be denied, are important cultural artefacts and, in societies like our own, we would be quite at sea without them. The Dictionary probably reflects our need for orderliness and apparent system rather than a real need for an inventory of word meanings. The most the dictionary can do perhaps is to 'supply hints and associations that will relate the unknown to something known'.

In a later chapter we will be considering whether, independently of dictionaries, there is anything intrinsic in the nature of words which enables us to use them reliably. For the present, we will explore some of the wider ramifications of words and their use.

Notes and Suggested Further Reading

Different points of view taken by linguists are illustrated by the following articles: (1) H.A. Gleason: 'The relations of lexicography and grammar', and (2) U. Weinreich: 'Lexicographic definition in descriptive semantics'. Both articles are to be found in F.W. Householder and S. Saporta (eds.): Problems in Lexicography *(Bloomington, Indiana, 1967). Weinreich's views have been particularly influential. A useful set of articles also is reprinted in Part Four of V.P. Clark, P.A. Eschholz and A.F. Rosa (eds.):* Language *(2nd edn., New York, 1977).*

For a history of dictionaries the reader would find D.W.T. Starnes and G.E. Noyes: The English Dictionary from Cawdrey to Johnson 1604-1755 *(Chapel Hill, 1946) interesting. See also the fascinating book by R.L. Collison:* A History of Foreign-Language Dictionaries *(London, 1982). For a readable human portrait of dictionary making, a biography of James Murray, one of the pioneers of the Oxford English Dictionary, see the book by his daughter, of the same surname:* Caught in a Web of Words *(London, 1978).*

A more recent introductory book on language, much more recent than Sapir's, is Bolinger and Sears' Aspects of Language *(3rd Edn., New York, 1981).*

The most recent survey is A. Akmajian, R.A. Demers and R.M. Harnish: Linguistics: An Introduction to Language and Communication *(2nd Edn., Cambridge, Mass., 1984).*

3

THE USE OF WORDS

WHAT HAPPENS WHEN WE TALK

George Orwell was himself convinced, and convinced many of his readers equally, that the decline of a nation and a civilisation is tied up with the decline of the language. What he called 'political dialects' have overwhelmed our language with clichés, lifeless ready-made phrases, and a tendency to glue these together to form what passes for genuine utterance and significant prose. Language is such, Orwell noted, that if you don't keep your wits about you these ready-made prefabricated phrases will come rushing in and do your thinking for you.

> 'They will construct your sentences for you — even think your thoughts for you to a certain extent — and at need they will perform the important service of partially concealing your meaning even from yourself'.

How is it possible, you may be wondering, that words can do our thinking for us when each of us has individual control over the language we use?

One simple answer is that language is primarily *social*, not individual. In other words, language is rooted in human communication; and the forces that regulate language are, again primarily, social. For language to develop in the individual, that individual needs to be in constant communication with at least one other human individual. I say at least one other, because there exist several well-documented cases of pairs of children, usually twins, who have grown up in isolated areas or with neglectful or deaf parents. Otto Jespersen mentions the case of an Icelandic girl who lived on a remote farm in northern Iceland. The girl used to converse with her twin brother in an unintelligible language. The parents decided to send the brother away, and shortly thereafter he died. They tried to teach their daughter Icelandic but finally gave up on her. Instead they learnt her language, as did the rest of the family and some of their friends. Her elder brother even had to translate the catechism for her. The girl would have grown up speaking normal Icelandic if only her family, as Jespersen points out, had not been foolish enough to go along with her language idiosyncrasies into adolescence. Indeed, we all accommodate very considerably to the language habits of others, especially within the family circle. It is quite common, for instance, for severely deaf children not to be diagnosed as such, until they go to school, by which time the language learning capacity of the child is already on the wane. We are very much dependent on each other when it comes to learning to talk, and we are not exaggerating when we say: no social relationships, no language.

We cannot remain satisfied with such a one-sided answer as this, however. For we can be sure that language is also rooted in the human individual. The biological and cognitive processes may need to be triggered by the social environment and also nourished by that same environment, but these processes are autonomous and subject in large measure to the unfolding of the nervous system and the 'psycho-biology' of the individual. No amount of social intercourse will overcome severe defects in the brain and central nervous system, for all that a normal environment may compensate to some extent.

Herein then lies a paradox: language is both socially and individually determined. So far, there is no equation which embraces both the individual and the social environment. Much is known about the interface between the two, but we possess only faint ideas of how social the individual needs to be, and how dependent on the creative energies of the individual a society must also be.

Take, for example, our 'popular science' conception of communication. Communication, most people are satisfied to suppose, resembles a kind of signalling dialogue between individuals; for simplicity's sake usually confined to two individuals. One individual says ('encodes') something, and the receiving individual is supposed to 'decode' what has been said. This latter individual, in turn, encodes a response, and the first individual decodes this response. In this manner, communication is supposed to take place. Leaving aside the large question mark against the notion of 'code' in this context, since it does not concern us here, we are still left to imagine that some 'content' in somebody's mind or brain is encoded as a message to someone other, who then decodes the message to determine what this content might possibly be.

The implication of all this is that something real — pieces of meaning — are actually transmitted. The coding is said to be by means of signs, which embody both 'form' (the sounds, or the letters) and 'content'. In fact, the sounds that we make, and the marks we make on paper, are only devices for making communication easier and more efficient, provided we revise our more simplistic standpoint and recognise that *nothing*, no message, in a 'loaded with *content*' sense, is actually transmitted. Our vocal and graphic gestures are merely the outward symptoms of a much more truly remarkable *and* observable phenomenon: the matching of separate consciousnesses, the confluence of separate human beings. When we communicate, we set in motion a train of events, verbal gestures which can be vocal, or marks on a sheet of paper. In this way, the person I am communicating with becomes endowed with the possibility of having comparable thoughts or impressions to mine.

Communication is the result rather of a kind of sympathetic resonance. No content, I repeat, is 'transmitted' between individuals as such. The sounds, marks on paper, and gestures are the aids by which this resonance is established. The rules of language — the mastery of these sounds, marks or gestures — are precise and efficient enough to ensure that this resonance sometimes appears spontaneous.

The French philosopher Merleau-Ponty was right in dismissing as illusion the experience of two-way communication. Indeed, none of us would be able to understand the most commonplace of utterances, the simplest of texts, if they did not arouse in us impressions, thoughts, and sensations that were already ours: 'It is within a world already spoken and speaking that we think'. In speaking or writing we do little more than take up a position within the world of meanings.

Merleau-Ponty's approach has received independent support from neurophysiology. The older model of transmitter-receiver has been found wanting in that quarter too. The speaker-hearer signalling model simply does not fit the facts observed. A hearer, it now appears, does not simply 'hear', 'decode', as many linguists and others once believed, and some still believe. The hearer, it seems, reconstructs, replicates within his own nervous system and perceptions the speech of the speaker. It is quite certain that if this reconstructive capacity is by as much as a hair's breadth impaired, either genetically or through brain damage, speech will be defective and comprehension seriously hampered. A severely deaf child, for instance, will not develop his natural capacity for speech without positive aid, because there is little or nothing for this capacity to build on. Speech is perceived not as a result of plain receptive hearing, but by motor articulations simulated in the hearer. The hearer somehow picks up the sensation that someone is speaking, and then has to construct a whole series of 'models', one after another, but in a matter of micro-seconds, before he or she finds an adequate model. This is not a completely abstract, cognitive type of activity. The hearer has to reconstruct in terms of actual speech articulation and kinaesthetic function — in ordinary language, the hearer has to be able to say the incoming words to himself. This process, it appears, mediates between incoming sensations and the event psychologists and philosophers call perception — I recognize that somebody is addressing me, and — ah! — wants to know the way to the nearest Underground station.

Communication is thus, quite literally, a going out towards the other, a process of matching. Communication becomes most complete only when the gap between speaker and hearer, with all the unimaginably complex neurophysiological and cognitive activity this entails, is reduced to vanishing point.

How then, you may well ask, *does* a message get from one person to another, from a speaker to a hearer? If we are not transmitting meanings, coded messages, or 'content' of some kind, what *is* going on?

The answer would seem to be that our organisms have developed various devices which enable the 'recipient' of a message to reconstruct the content of the message being 'transmitted'. The transmissions are not actual messages then, but *signs* of various kinds. These signs may be divided into three types: *vocal*, *graphic* and *gestural*. The vocal signs are the ones we have already mentioned, and involve the cognitive activity of the hearer as well as the neurophysiology of the human ear. The graphic signs impinge on the eye, the most familiar ones being marks on paper, print or handwriting; but pictures and drawings, especially in pre-literate cultures, are equally important. Gestures are movements, and involve kinaesthesis as well as sight. Gestures are a constant accompaniment to speech, and speech itself can arguably be shown to be a complex sequence of gestures, associated with our speech organs: mainly the lips, tongue, larynx, soft palate, and the nasal, oral and pharyngeal cavities. Sign languages, the languages used among deaf-mutes, are completely gestural.

Communication occurs through one or more of these channels — aural, graphic or gestural — the whole time. When we hear a piece of music, and feel that it does something for us, 'communicates' something to us, we are interpreting a range and sequence of signs. The same applies when we similarly respond to a drawing, a picture, pottery, dance, film, or any other form of art. My use of the term 'art' is intended to embrace 'popular' as well as 'fine' art. Clearly, an impressive amount of communication is occurring at a packed open-air rock concert, certainly not less than in the more rarefied ambience of the recital hall.

The signs associated with language are evidently at least in large degree different from those associated with other media. They have a biologically determined base, and are thus universal in their specificity. For instance, all languages have noun and verb phrases, interrogative forms, transitive and intransitive verbs, tense frameworks, and much else. They are also recursive and cyclic, perhaps reflecting the operation of the central nervous system itself. This 'base' can be compared to submerged part of an iceberg, and is thus very large in comparison to the part that sticks up above the surface. The part that we see (or rather, hear), the part that is sticking up above the surface, is what makes each language different from each other. Here, the differences are caused mainly, perhaps entirely, by cultural factors, the most crucial part being the words we use, those relatively permanent and all-pervasive cultural artefacts we spoke about in the first chapter. We shall see, later, how words serve as mediators of culture and provide us with our meanings, which at the same time are the meanings shared by the wider speech community.

To return then to our original question: What happens when we talk? One answer seems to be that, in a very real sense, *we become the words we use.* Our individual histories start from the time when we learn the use of language, and our memories will seldom antedate that learning. When we talk about 'mastery' of language, we are referring to something rather superficial, the acquisition of rhetorical competence; an important acquisition, no doubt, analogous rather to the cultivation of etiquette and good taste than to any fundamental grasp of language, which our unconscious biological processes have taken complete care of, provided they have not been impeded.

Notes and Suggested Further Reading

Otto Jespersen's Language: Its Nature, Development and Origin *(London, 1922), again a vintage work, is a mine of information, much of it still of interest to today's reader, specialist and layman alike.*

The conception of communication goes back to the invention of sophisticated signalling systems, and especially to the telegraph. This kind of 'model' was reinforced by Ferdinand de Saussure in the early years of this century, and maintained by many scholars, prominent among whom have been Roman Jakobson, Umberto Eco, Julia Kristava, and others.

Maurice Merleau-Ponty's views are especially to be found in his Phenomenology of Perception *(London, 1962).*

21

4

HOW DID WORDS ORIGINATE?

Much has happened since the time when, in 1866, the Linguistic Society of Paris expressly banned any further speculation on the origins of language as a waste of time. In those days language was believed to be simply one among the many attributes of human beings. Today, language is reckoned to be the basis of everything human, and some are of the opinion that a discussion of the origin of language is really an inquiry into the origin of origins.

Although, even now, it is impossible to say with any certainty how language actually developed, we are at least in a better position to understand how non-human beings, by dint of acquiring language, became human.

But first, the difficulties.

One of these difficulties is that, despite what might have been expected, the languages of primitive peoples are found to be just as complex as the languages of more advanced societies. Only the vocabularies of the languages of primitive peoples tend to be smaller, partly of course because they do not have access to the vast range of man-made objects and concepts that surround us. And then there are the culture differences. English has more than a dozen basic words for colour, but some languages have colour terms only for white, black and red. Jalé, a language of the New Guinea Highlands, appears to have only two: one depicting brightness, and the other dullness. This does not mean that the speakers of these languages are partially colour-blind. On the contrary, they can indicate fine shades of colour distinction if they need to, by making figurative connections with plants, birds, and such like. Moreover, poverty of vocabulary in one area may well be compensated by a bewildering wealth of terms in other areas. Claude Lévi-Strauss (*The Savage Mind*) tells of a Westerner arriving among an African tribe and wanting to learn the language. Her informant-teachers found it perfectly natural, at an elementary stage in the programme of instruction, to collect a large number of botanical specimens, the names of which they told her as they showed them to her. The problem for the visitor very quickly became not the language, but her inability to distinguish plant forms, let alone remember their names. Plants had never been her particular interest, whereas the natives took such an interest for granted. Even a child, she later discovered, could know the names of literally hundreds of plants. None of her hosts could realize that it was not the words but the plants that were baffling her.

We cannot however infer that, since the languages of primitive peoples are just as complicated as ours, the languages of early man were equally complex. The stone technology of the now extinct Tasmanians, as we know it, may have been less advanced in many respects than that of Neanderthal Man who roamed the earth some 100,000 or more years ago, but the language (or what we know of it) of these Tasmanians was just as developed as the invaders' language — English. This is a point that needs to be stressed. The most primitive and the most 'advanced' languages used today are of the same age; they are contemporary. Their differences can be accounted for only by the different cultures of the societies that use these languages. We may pride ourselves on the sheer verbal abundance and the repertoire of expressiveness of a language like English, and would be inclined to look a down on a language like Eskimo, which does not even have a properly developed system of numerals. But we shouldn't forget that the Eskimo would not exchange his language for English, especially if he wanted to go on living the life of an Eskimo. To start with, English has far too few words for snow and ice, compared with Eskimo, which has scores of words, all necessary for his survival and well-being.

It is now thought more likely — although this must remain to some extent speculation — that language developed gradually, and only reached its full development with *Homo Sapiens* some 30,000 to 35,000 years ago. The fossil record shows that early Modern Man was well distributed around the globe by this comparatively late date; and was even to be found in geographically isolated Australia and Tasmania. It seems probable that language *originated* much earlier than this, and there is wide consensus that the earliest stone technology and language developed hand in hand. The reason for supposing this is that the fossil record and the development of human technology are parallel. We know that the creatures who left behind the earliest known series of human fossils, some one million or more years ago, stood erect, and some chipped pebbles; and we have no reason to suppose that their brain was of the wrong structure or too small to support a fully fledged language. It is more probable however that the build-up of language was gradual, and that the abstract classificatory structure and recursive systems of grammar we recognise as our own language only came in with *Homo Sapiens*, which in palaeontological terms would have been relatively quite recent (not more than a mere 35,000 years ago). We may also be sure that the development of social relations and ritual was an essential adjunct of language formation, and particularly of the specific ways in which we handle discourse and manage our word stocks. The time is almost ripe, perhaps already ripe, for a multi-parametric model which would enable us to calibrate and relate specific language developments to the fossil record.

So far we have only touched on the origins of language. What about the origin of *words*? Can we say anything useful about that?

Until a few years ago, one would have had to answer no. All we could have said with any degree of certainty was that words are, at the level of sound, indistinguable parts of the flow of speech, and that the farther we go back in time it would usually be more difficult to recognise them as individual words. Even today, there are many languages — French is one very choice example — where it would be very difficult to impossible without the help of written language to analyse the components of even short sentences. *Qu'est ce qu'il y a?* ('What's going on?'), for instance, could be said to contain up to seven words, depending on how you count them? But the French speaker pronounces this sentence as if it were one word only: [keskilya]. In all languages, however, phrases and whole sentences consist of word-forms bound together in sequence by intonation and other factors. Individual words, even in languages like English or Chinese where word boundaries are clearly marked, lose much of their definition in normal rapid speech. Listen to the actual way an ordinary piece of talk sounds. In a question like

What would you have gone and done if you had been me?

Only the words *what, you* (first occurrence), *gone, done* and *me* have anything like their full pronunciation. The remaining words are as if swallowed up or at any rate much reduced:

WHAT w'd YOU 'v GONE'n DONE 'f y'd b'n ME?

In many pre-literate languages it is possible to identify individual words with the assistance of informants, but the words may look very different from the ones with which we are familiar, and their forms will often be unstable, and subject to a fair amount of contextual variation. The latter occur even in 'sophisticated' languages like English. If you listen to the conventional greetings 'good morning' or 'good night' you will seldom hear these phrases spoken with their full phonetic value.

We have of course no way of knowing for sure whether Neanderthal Man was conscious of words in the same way as Modern Man. But the probability is that he was not, and that earlier phases of human language were less well lexically developed, that phrases and sentences came out as unanalysable and unstable wholes. The fact that chimpanzees and gorillas have been shown to be capable of partial learning and manipulation of the lexicon in no way proves that early man was in possession of a like degree of attainment. If Neanderthal Man were still around today, it is likely that, reared in our midst, he would in time learn modern languages almost as well as anyone else, just as he would learn to use modern tools. He might even learn to read newspapers, and watch television.

A clue to the origin of actual words is to be found in the intriguing ideas of the French ethnologist André Leroi-Gourhan. In a rather crude nutshell, Léroi-Gourhan's theory is that speech and writing have entirely separate origins, but that from quite early times, in fact from the Upper (or Late) Palaeolithic period, towards the close of the last Ice Age, human vocal and graphic expression have been interrelated. Both activities in their different ways, speaking and writing, says Léroi-Gourhan, have arisen from a common aptitude for extracting the symbolic from the confused world of sensation. Language, he goes on to argue, was born of an intellectual coupling of sound and line. The earliest known cave paintings and rock carvings are abstract and rhythmic, matching the equally abstract and rhythmic succession of sounds that go to make up the speech continuum. Only after the lapse of a considerable period of time, some tens of thousands of years, did graphic expression become 'representational', reaching its fullest 'classical' phase of realism in the Magdalenian cave paintings (the best known being those at Lascaux in the Dordogne and at Altamira in Northern Spain) between 11,000 and 8,000 B.C.

These early cave drawings, even at their most vividly representational, are always highly formalised, almost stereotyped sometimes, and above all, are repeated not only within the same mural setting, but from one location to another. As such, they have long puzzled archaeologists and art historians. We can in fact make real sense of these Palaeolithic designs, argues Leroi-Gourhan, only if we regard them as a pre-linear form of writing. Not a transient, makeshift form of writing, let it be noted, but a powerful and highly developed system with a very long history of its own, reaching back for all we know into the Neanderthal past. If this view is correct, in by far the longest segment of the history of mankind, pre-civilised man worked with, and at, forms of mental representation which have become alien and incomprehensible to civilised man with his linear, phonetically informed writing. According to such a view, the cave paintings would have been the non-linear'texts' for an entire mythology, a whole 'literature' of ritual narrative and epic. These 'mythograms' as Léroi-Gourhan calls them, would have been 'read', just as surely as the present-day Australian Aboriginal reads from his primitively inscribed *churinga*. The first linear *speech*-related writing, such as we find in Ancient China, Egypt of the Pharaohs, Sumer, and the Indus Valley, as well as among the somewhat later Mayas, developed only with the coming of agriculture and pastoralism, of city states, reflecting the need for calendric records, inventories, tabulations, oracles, and in general the greater complexities and need for technical precision engendered by settled societies.

If we situate the history of the word along the interface of vocal and graphic expression we will be inclined to see the word as having a long and gradually unfolding genesis, all the way from the opaque, but sometimes graphically vivid, mythograms of some tens of millennia ago, by way of the ideograms and pictograms of Neolithic civilisations, through to the most precise logic and most sophisticated diction of our own age. The words we use everyday — our chairs, tables, trees, houses and gardens, our tools and favoured objects, our rainbows and sunsets — are still just as mysterious as the 'mythograms' in the caves of Lascaux. It is just that their mystery mostly eludes us, particularly in modern times, when our consumerism conspires to shield us altogether from the enigmatic and extraordinary world that surrounds us.

Notes and Suggested Further Reading

Profitable reading at this stage would include Chapter 10 of Bolinger and Sear's Aspects of Language *pp. 231-235 (see Notes, etc. to Chapter 2 for detailed reference).*

If you read French, even not too fluently, you should try to come by a copy of A. Leroi-Gourhan's: Le Geste et La Parole *(Paris, 1964). The works by Sapir and Jespersen also have sections which deal with the origins of language.*

You could also read Chapter 2 of Akmajian, Demers and Harnish Linguistics.

5

HOW DO WORDS

CHANGE THEIR MEANING?

Readers need no reminding that some words in our language have undergone changes of meaning. Until a few years ago, for example, *gay* meant predominantly 'full of joy', 'exuberantly cheerful' or some such, but nowadays it is quite difficult to use the word without implying 'homosexual'. *Rock* nowadays refers to a genre of pop music. *Punk* once meant various things, including 'prostitute', 'a fungus', 'Chinese incense', and more recently a 'worthless person'. It is only in very recent times that *punk* has acquired its current and predominant meaning. Thirty years ago, *jet set*, if it had meant anything at all, would have suggested perhaps a chess or draughts set made of lignite. At about the same period a *satellite* would have been taken to mean a 'dependent nation or state, a dependency'. People used to talk about countries in the Soviet bloc as satellites of the Soviet Union. It was only during the 1960s, with the advent of the space age, that the more familiar meaning of satellite started to eclipse its political meaning, to the extent that today a person would risk being incompletely understood if he or she were to talk of Czechoslovakia as a one-time Soviet satellite. One could go on.... Instead, we will ask ourselves why it is that only certain words change their meaning, and not all.

The answer, as if the reader hadn't already anticipated, is not that simple.

It will have been observed that all the examples just cited are words that reflect contemporary preoccupations and ways of life. And yet, only some of the key words of today have been subjected to this kind of change. Why? The short answer is that change of meaning in existing words is only one of the ways in which new meanings can be achieved. We shall be having a look at some of the other ways in the next two chapters, the two main ways being (1) coinage of new words (e.g. *disc jockey*, by putting the hitherto unrelated words *disc* and *jockey* together as a single word compound) and (2) the borrowing of words from other languages, including 'dead' languages like Greek and Latin.

The less easily satisfied reader will already have noticed however that there is still a very large body of English words unaccounted for; words which we need in our everyday, but which have neither been freshly coined, nor borrowed from another language, nor have recently changed their meaning. In fact, on closer inspection of the dictionary, it will be seen that very few words in the English language, with the exception of recent coinages or recent borrowings, have not at some time or other undergone a change of meaning, often a *series* of changes at different times in their history.

Words that seem *not* to have changed their meaning are so ancient that there are no written records to indicate when they last changed their meaning. One such case is *ox*. The stem form *oxen-* is so old that Sanskrit, the Classical language of the Brahmin priests of India and a very distant cousin of English, contains the closely related stem form *ukṣán-*. (Both stem-forms *-oxen* and *ukṣán-* are descended from a hypothetical 'Indo-European' form **uksin-*.) We can be sure nevertheless (even though we do not know the full details of the change) that at some time before *uksin-* became *ukṣán-* in India and *oksen* (i.e. *oxen*) in Western Europe — in Neolithic times that is, perhaps as long ago as eight thousand years, or even earlier — the denotation had at some time changed from a kind of wild cattle to a *domesticated* gelded bull; for the straightforward reason that it was in the early Neolithic era, as we

29

know from archaeology, that animals were first domesticated.

This brings us round, if by an unexpected route, to the point that all changes of meaning accompany changes in outlook, way of life (culture), technology and taste. Indeed, word meaning and cultural manifestation are so closely intertwined as to be indistinguishable from each other. This is something we should never lose sight of, as writers like Owen Barfield have been constantly reminding us. To take a single example: the concept *gravity* underwent radical change in the half century between Galileo and Newton, from just 'heaviness' to 'the degree of intensity with which one body is affected by the attraction of gravitation exercised by another body'. The *meaning* of the word *gravity* changed in proportion to that of the scientific concept, but the change was so automatic that it did not attract any particular attention at the time.

In the same century, a whole range of word-concepts which had been impregnated with medieval cosmology changed their meanings also. Before the 'scientific revolution' of the seventeenth century, a word like *atmosphere*, a word then only recently borrowed from Greek, meant 'a kind of breath which the Earth exhaled from itself'. Note the use of the capital letter for 'Earth', suggesting a living being. Before Galileo, all the stars and planets, as well as the Moon and the Earth were considered to be living bodies, which had an 'influence' on each other and particularly on human beings (the word *influenza* is from this particular 'influence'). Even the word *test*, that Francis Bacon made so much of, is derived from a Latin word *testa*, an earthenware pot in which the alchemist made his alloys.

Where do these changes originate, and how are such changes propagated? Here certainly are two questions which we should keep distinct. The reasons why will become apparent later.

First, the question of the *origins* of meaning change. It must certainly be that many, if not most, new meanings originated amongst ordinary people, anonymously. The reason for this is that every time a word, or idiom, is used, the meaning is (however infinitesimally) changed. This is not entirely because people are vague about the meanings of words, as enshrined in the dictionary, or because people have a tendency to ignore their grammatical status (e.g. taking the noun *chair*, and using it as a verb, as in 'to chair a meeting' — a meaning which today everyone accepts, but which is still not officially admitted by such dictionaries as *The Shorter Oxford Dictionary*); but for the very simple reason that real-life contexts are not generally repeatable, and real-life people *apply* words differently in different situations.

Second, the question of *propagation*. Speech is the primary means of spreading changes in meaning around the speech community, and undoubtedly many, probably most, of the 'quantum' changes recorded by the historical dictionary are due simply to speakers adopting new meanings by reproducing what they have heard others says. Mostly these changes are limited to a small group of people. Here in particular, we have the growth of 'slang' in its true sense (as opposed to its confusion with 'colloquialism') as an in-group sort of language. Sometimes, but only seldom, slang seeps out into the language as a whole. Or the changes may be ephemeral: they may come and go like the seasons. But a small proportion of these changes become fixed, usually through somebody's writing them down.

A period of massive change in English came in the sixteenth century, when the High Renaissance, already on the wane in the country of its origin — Italy — reached England. There was felt to be a need for many thousands of new ideas, techniques, new ways of doing things, new objects, so that words were borrowed wholesale from Italian, French, Spanish, Latin, and especially, Greek. Many foreign and classical words were anglicised, and through their use by writers, scholars and men of science, entered the English lexicon. This was the age of Humanism, of the age in which people cast off their medieval traditions and became recognisably 'modern', with preoccupations not so different from our own.

A key agent of semantic change during this period was Shakespeare. The English language would of course have changed, and indeed was changing, regardless. But it was Shakespeare who gave his particular personal stamp to an astonishing range of instances. Words like *create, religion* and *magic*, for example, had been previously used only in the spheres of religion or superstition. From now on they are applied to human beings. Antony becomes the 'noble ruin' of Cleopatra's 'magic' and Romeo speaks of 'the devout religion of mine eye'. Under Shakespeare's genius words like *amazement, critical, fashionable, generous, majestic, obscene, pedant, pious, sanctimonious*, and many more, suddenly appear to take on their modern meanings. Shakespeare even plays a semantic part in the relations between the sexes. Women cease to be allegorical symbols and become creatures of real flesh and blood. As Barfield has said,

'A careful study of Shakespeare reveals him as the probable author of a great part of the modern meanings of several words which are practically key-terms to whole areas of modern thought...... there is a very real sense, humiliating as it may seem, in which what we generally venture to call our feelings are really Shakespeare's "meaning".'

The different meanings of the same word that accrue over the centuries are known as *polysemy*. They can be compared to the branches of a tree. The analogy is good, to the extent that some shoots are more vigorous than others, while at the other extreme some branches wither altogether and die. The latter are the 'obsolete' meanings included in dictionaries like *The Oxford English Dictionary*. To take but one example, *bureau* (originally the word was spelt *burel*) once meant' a coarse woollen cloth', but through its use as a furniture covering, came to mean 'a writing table', and eventually an 'office' or 'organisation'. If we take the word *humour*, a word originally borrowed from Old French and Latin, and in its primary modern sense a peculiarly English word, we can reconstruct something like Figure 1.

It can be seen that the three unrelated current meanings of HUMOUR are explicable only in terms of a branching ancestry of meaning changes, traceable back to medieval French and, ultimately, Latin. The primary modern meaning, encapsulated in the phrase *sense of humour*, is enclosed in a frame to highlight its dominance. The meaning 'mood, humour' can only easily be used in set phrases like 'good-humoured' or as the verb 'to humour (someone)'. *Aqueous humour* is a specialised meaning which by chance has survived into modern anatomical usage. In passing, we might note that the Latin word *humour* as used in

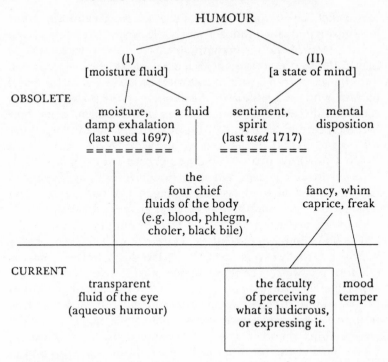

Figure 1

Roman times had only the first meaning, 'moisture, fluid', and no trace at all of the psychological sense (II). Even the four humours owe their origin to a medieval revival of Platonic Greek thought, and fragments of Hippocrates.

That branch of linguistic science which is concerned with the origins of words is known as *etymology*. This science came into being when it was believed that words did have actual discrete origins, in the sense that they came into being all of a piece at some particular time in the past. Descendants from these origins had fallen from grace. The Greek word *etymos* from which etymology is derived means 'true', and the implication was that words did have a true and original signification.

    Linguists and lexicographers today no longer subscribe to any

33

such belief. The earliest recorded use of a word cannot possibly be the original since (linear) writing is a comparatively recent development. Although in common parlance the word etymology may still be used, etymology as a science has long been incorporated into the wider framework of historical linguistics. The historical linguist, with the assistance of the philologist (the student of texts) can not only reliably trace the history of word-forms from their earliest recorded occurrence to the present day, but can sometimes reconstruct hypothetical forms as they would have occurred in a Proto-Indo-European language. (Proto-Indo-European is believed to be the antecedent of most present day European languages and of some Asian languages, like Old Persian and Avestan, Sanskrit and the northern languages of India.)

The reconstructed Proto-Indo-European word for 'wolf' is the unlikely looking *wḷqʷos. It has to be so, in order to account for what are virtually certain to be the various historical descendants (all meaning 'wolf'): (Latin) *lupus*, (Greek) *lúkos*, (Germanic) *wulf/ wolf*, (Russian) *volk*, (Sanskrit) *vr̥kas*. To provide a proper account of the sound changes involved would require quite a bit of technical detail and space, but we could just note in passing: (1) the third sound in the Indo-European must be q^w (or k^w) because otherwise we couldn't have a *p* in the same position in Latin; by a process known as 'labialisation'; (2) the second sound (which is a 'vocalic' as in English [teibl] = 'table' is hypothesised since sometimes the sounds in derivative Indo-European languages are -*ul*-/-*ol*- and sometimes *lu*-, and there is actually a 'rhotacised' equivalent of *l* in Sanskrit, namely *r* (rhotacism is the not infrequent substitution of *r* for sounds like *l* and *s*).

But now let us turn to the *semantics* of sound change. We have seen that new meanings have cropped up frequently, even in quite recent times. Although it may sometimes appear, from the dictionary, that a new meaning has overlaid and ousted an earlier meaning, this may be only appearance, not reality. What usually happens is that the new and the old meanings coexist, sometimes for considerable periods of time, until the old meaning either takes on an existence in its own right, or until the old meaning drops out. In the case of dropping out, this is seldom final and irrevocable, as words usually go on existing in regional dialects.

For example, the word *starve* once meant 'to die from hunger, cold or grief, or disease' (compare German *sterben* 'to die'). In Shakespeare's time the semantics of the word *starve* split into two branches: (1) 'to die of hunger' (2) 'to die of cold'. The former is the only meaning to have survived into contemporary standard English. The latter, however, survives in a hyperbolical sense in many Northern areas of England, where 'to be starved' would mean primarily 'to be nearly dead or numb with cold'. In British English the word *turnpike*, while not exactly obsolete, is mainly of historical interest, whereas in the United States *turnpike* is a living word, actually applied to certain types of road. Similarly, *journeyman*, in Britain understood mainly by the social historian, has a very real and current sense for a speaker of American English.

To round off our excursion, a brief word about the mechanics of semantic change.

Firstly, meanings do not change in the same way as organisms change; in other words, meaning X does not *turn into* Y. What happens is that one meaning *replaces* another. It is a fairly well established fact that, for a period, which may be very short or quite long, the older or more conservative meaning and a newer innovative meaning co-exist side by side. Eventually, the new meaning supersedes the older one altogether, in the following (simplified) manner:

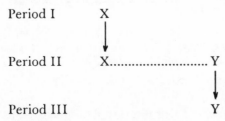

Period I   X

Period II   X......................... Y

Period III   Y

A brief inspection of a historical dictionary, especially *The Oxford English Dictionary* will provide many an example of this process of replacement. The older form either dies out completely, or becomes a rare, usually 'learned' or literary specimen, or maintains a reduced existence in dialect, or alternatively, survives only in set phrases.

A good example to take is the word *enthusiasm*, which was borrowed from Greek in the late sixteenth century. The first recorded use of the word in an English context is in Spenser, where the word is actually spelt in its original Greek form and orthography.

The word has had four different senses in English: (1) possession by a god; poetic or prophetic frenzy, (2) poetical fervour; impassioned mood, (3) fancied inspiration; misdirected religious emotion, (4) rapturous intensity of feeling in favour of a person, principle, or cause. Only sense (4) survives into Modern English. Diagrammatically, we can represent these rival senses as in Figure 2:

ENTHUSIASM

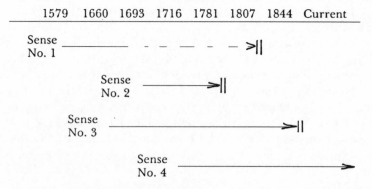

| 1579 | 1660 | 1693 | 1716 | 1781 | 1807 | 1844 | Current |

Note: Dotted line indicates that the sense continues to be used, but only with an archaic connotation (The last recorded archaic usage for Sense No. 1 is 1807). Double verticals indicate the last date of recorded use.

These changes of meaning, or rather, replacements of meaning, are controlled less by linguistic than by social factors. Studies in North America, England, and elsewhere in the 1960s and 1970s showed how phonological and, to a more limited extent, morphological features of the language were subject to change, dependent on a range of different social or other non-linguistic factors. These factors were found to include age, sex, socioeconomic status, and considerations such as the degree of formality, all the way from casual conversation to highly formalised exercises like reading lists of words. William Labov and those associated with his approach have confirmed that these processes are unconscious, outcomes being predictable not in terms of individuals but of statistical distribution. It is interesting to note that some of these changes are ongoing and that they exhibit polarity between 'conservativism' and 'innovativeness'. However, the 'socio-linguistic' processes themselves are exceedingly complex, with different individual words having the same phonological profile and showing different rates of change, with some exhibiting a higher degree of conservatism than others.

For this kind of sociolinguistic variation to show up in semantics in such minute detail would be expecting far too much, because of the vast and unstable range of word meaning. Also, at the level of words, form (word shape) and sense (meaning) interact with each other in curious ways.

To reduce the matter to its most elementary level: once two words begin to *look*, or *sound* alike, their meanings affect each other. Word-pairs like *scare* and *scarify*, *militate* and *mitigate*, *vague* and *vagaries*, *appraise* and *apprise* are frequently confused, despite their wide differences in meaning, purely because of the similarity of the word shape in each case. And pairs like *complementary* and *complimentary*, or *principle* and *principal*, can be the bugbear of even the most fastidious. This phenomenon of contagion is well recognised, and has been probed quite extensively, down to the recognition that words that have the same form (*homonyms*), by historical or other coincidence, will develop somewhat different meanings, or alternatively, one of the forms will drop out. Instances of 'homonymic clash' are legion. This process is well illustrated in English homonymic clashes brought about by the coexistence of two different but related languages — Old English (Anglo-Saxon) and Old Scandinavian (Old Norse) — during the early Middle Ages. One such instance is *gate* 'entrance' (from Old English *geat*) and *gate* 'road, street' (from Old Norse *gata*). In early times the words were used interchangeably, but by Chaucer's time their meanings had become as separate and distinct as they are today. Since the fourteenth century the second of these meanings (i.e. 'road, street') has dropped out, except in street and place names like *Broadgate*, *Fishergate*, *Highgate*, etc.

The mechanisms underlying the interaction of word shapes and word meanings are as yet incompletely understood; though there is mounting evidence that below the level of the actual word there exist 'morphosemantic' components which are relatively stable, and underlie the full lexical word as such. The French linguist Pierre Guiraud has done much work on this interchangeability between word shape and word meaning (morphosemantics), and it has been followed up by others, including the present author.

One curious facet of the morphosemantic structure of words is that area of historical semantics known as *popular* or *folk etymology*. The interchangeability of word shape and word meaning has made it possible for the usage of the ordinary speaker to reflect a different scheme of relationship between word shape and word meaning from that of official or literate speech, and at times a tendency for the popular usage to replace the latter.

There are numerous examples. Many of them arise from popular shifts in word boundaries. *Orange* began life as the Spanish *narancia* and arose, in English, as the result of popular confusion between *a norange* (from the Spanish *naranja*) and *an orange*. (Other Examples include *newt* (from *an ewt*), *adder* (from Fr. *naddre*), and many more). An importation like *asparagus* becomes *sparrow grass* in ordinary speech. The Elizabethan *bufetier* (from French *buffet*) becomes the modern English *beefeater*. French *surloin* 'above the loin' becomes, by folk etymology and not by any legendary capricious conferring of a knighthood, *sirloin*. An ostensibly alien mouthful *Eleanor Infanta of Castile*, the queen of Edward I, becomes in the course of time the *Elephant and Castle*. Work that one out!

Finally, the most difficult obstacle in the path of any sociolinguistic study of lexical and semantic variance is the overriding importance of context. It was I.A. Richards who first drew the attention of the wider public to the fact that words cannot be studied in isolation from *context*. He even went one stage further: to the extreme claim that a word meaning is no more than a function of the context in which it occurs, a word acquiring what

Richards called a 'delegated efficacy', by courtesy of the linguistic context in which it occurs. In his *Philosophy of Rhetoric* Richards denied that words in isolation have any proper meaning. Only discourse as a whole, says Richards, carries meaning. Words possess meaning only through the abridgement of context: 'What a word means is the missing parts of the context from which it draws its delegated efficacy'. All that words can do is refer back to the missing parts of the context.

There is an undeniable degree of truth in Richard's thesis. Language functions as a whole; that we know for certain. And any comprehensive study of semantic change must make allowance for the role of context — not merely the juxtaposed words and phrases in which a particular word occurs, but the whole 'context of situation', including the collocational range of a word; which is something we will be looking at later on in this volume.

Notes and Suggested Further Reading

Bolinger and Sear's Chapter 10 should now be read to the end.

Also see Chapter 8 in Akmajian, Demers and Harnish (see Notes, etc. of Chapter 2 above for reference). There are numerous discussions of language change in Jespersen (see above for reference). You could also read Chaps 1-12 of W.P. Lehmann's Historical Linguistics: An Introduction *(New York, 1966). My own* Comparative Linguistics *(2nd Edn, London, 1974) is now out of print. See also Owen Barfield's* Poetic Diction *(2nd Edn. London, 1952).*

6

WORD BORROWING

In the last chapter we looked at one important way in which the vocabulary of a language is enriched and renewed. In this chapter and the next we will be considering still further ways. In the present chapter in particular, we shall be dealing with a phenomenon known as word borrowing.

Word borrowing varies in extent from language to language. Chinese is an example of a language which has borrowed very little from other languages, except in the rather specialised area of Buddhism. Japanese on the other hand has borrowed extensively, from Chinese, from Portuguese, from English and from many other languages. But perhaps the most 'indebted' language of all is English.

English has borrowed so extensively from other languages that it is not difficult to find whole pages in the dictionary which contain not a single word of Old English (Anglo-Saxon) origin. Indeed, it is not easy to find a page which consists of more than a fraction of originally English (i.e. Anglo- Saxon) words. What is the reason for this strange state of affairs, which has produced such a hybrid English vocabulary?

The main reason must be that for a period of between four and five hundred years, roughly from the age of Alfred the Great (ninth century) until the time of Chaucer (fourteenth century) speakers in England were largely bilingual. Stable bilingualism among a significant proportion of a population over a long period is a sure way of ensuring that sizeable numbers of foreign words and meanings will enter speakers' first or native language.

The first period of bilingualism was the result of the Scandinavian ('Viking') invasions. This bilingualism was probably confined to the Northern and Midland parts of the country but, with the establishment of Midland speech as the language standard in later medieval times, the words borrowed initially in the more northern parts spread throughout the whole country.

Hardly had this 'Scandinavian' period of bilingualism been consolidated when the Norman Conquest brought yet another foreign language — French — to England. This was a different kind of situation socially speaking. The English and Scandinavians had been people of similar background: farmers, herdsmen, and artisans of various kinds. But the Normans were all from the upper classes: gentry, high clergy, people of 'culture'. I use 'culture' in inverted commas because in fact the Normans on the whole were less learned, less literate and less artistic than their Saxon subjects. They looked down on, and for a time disregarded, all that did not originate in France. Otto Jespersen thought that it was from this time that the unfortunate British trait of class snobbery arose. Certainly, for a hundred and fifty years, or longer, the English ruling class and the English population as a whole spoke different languages: French (in its Old French and Anglo-Norman varieties) and English, respectively. This difference is so deeply ingrained in the language that groups of synonyms will tend to exhibit a two-nation complex. Suppose, for example, we look at some of the synonyms of courage, and arrange them in two columns. You may then see what I am driving at:

COURAGE

English	French
boldness	*bravery*
daring	*gallantry*

41

manliness   *valour*
pluck   *courage*
steadfastness   *heroism*
guts

I remember once, many years ago, puzzling over a neat way of capturing in words this difference, even a difference of 'atmosphere', in front a group of schoolboys, when one of them shot up his hand and asked: 'Aren't the ones in the French column the things you get medals for?' That just about summed it up. The English attributes, although just as 'courageous' as the French terms, hint at rawness, high spirits, spontaneity, inner fortitude. But, with the possible exception of *daring*, they are not exactly qualities that shine with martial splendour.

With the Renaissance came a whole flood of new concepts, techniques, manners and attitudes; fads also. The English language had been so inured to word borrowing by this time that foreign words were borrowed in profusion: from modern languages like French, Italian and Spanish, but also from Classical Latin and Greek. With the result that, by the end of the seventeenth century, English had acquired words it could well have done without. For instance, English has both *sleepwalker* and *somnambulist* (the difference between them being imperceptible); *shortsighted* and *myopic* (both can be used figuratively); *drunk*, *intoxicated*, and *inebriated*; and so forth. Many of the words borrowed during the sixteenth and seventeenth are either hopelessly specialised, improperly understood, or not understood at all by the ordinary speaker.

One of the strangest things of all about English is that it is still possible to construct fairly normal sentences using exclusively vocabulary taken from the separate strata (Old English, Norse, French, 'learned' or Latinate). The following samples are given for the record:

Old English:
The man in the wilderness asked of me
How many strawberries grow in the sea?
I answered him as I thought good,
As many red herrings as grow in the wood. (Anon)

French:
*People prefer travelling in groups particularly
during certain seasons despite very considerable reasons
favouring possible contrary arrangements.*

Latin(ate):
*Devastating` conflagrations, incinerating vast rural areas,
inflicted incalculable, irremediable destruction, exceeding prevalent
popular expectation.*

From the seventeenth century onwards, Britain embarked upon a long period of colonial expansion, which led to a growing influx of terms from exotic places: from the New World, from Africa, India, South-East Asia, and China, even from countries like Japan and Java where the colonial influence was felt only indirectly. Some of these words, like *okra, loquat, fan-tan*, and even *judo, veranda* and *orang-utan* are obviously exotic. But some have been so well domesticated that very few users of English would even suspect them of being foreign. *Punch*, for example, though it certainly can 'pack a punch', is actually borrowed from Northern India, having nothing to with impact, but with the five (Hindi *panch* 'five') ingredients of the beverage. *Compound*, in the sense of 'enclosure', is ultimately from Malay *kampong*, having been borrowed towards the end of the seventeenth century; having nothing to do with the other meanings of *compound*. *Godown*, meaning 'warehouse', is used in West Coast America and in South-East Asia, and is in no way related to 'going down', but probably to the Southern Indian (Telugu) word *gidangi*, 'place where goods lie around'. Even words which sound comical in English, and are used as terms of friendly ridicule, like *mugwump*, are not English in origin. This particular borrowing is from Algonquin, an American Indian language. Originally *mugwump* meant a 'great man', though already in a jocular sense.

The study of the actual process of word borrowing can be a fascinating occupation. When words are borrowed they usually undergo a change of clothing to fit them for their new habitat. Sometimes the sea change amounts to no more than what we might have expected. At the time when the word *ombrella* was borrowed from Italian, it meant in that sunny country a 'sun shade', but when it was naturalised as the English word *umbrella* it came to mean a 'rain shelter'. At other times the change is so far-reaching that we find ourselves up against irreconcilable cultural difference. If you were to look up the etymology of *school* you would find that it derives from a Greek word *skholē* meaning 'leisure' or 'spare time'. It was the Romans who were responsible for the drastic change of meaning, when they borrowed the word from the Greeks. For the no-nonsense Romans, 'school' was clearly harsh discipline and the very opposite of leisure or pleasure. It took three centuries of Modern European Enlightenment — all the way from Comenius to Matthew Arnold, Froebel and Montessori — to change attitudes, so that nowadays not every child resembles Shakespeare's whining schoolboy 'creeping like a snail unwillingly to school'.

The English have always held an ambivalent attitude towards the foreigner. The word *alien* (originally a French word) itself rings with this ambivalence. Once a word is recognised as 'alien' it will either be rejected as such, or if it is useful, kept in a kind of limbo. Such a word is *malaise*. If you look up this word in the Shorter Oxford you will notice that it is tagged as 'not naturalised, alien'. Yet, the word *malaise* has been around in English since 1768. It is admittedly not a commonly used word, because speakers have only occasional need for it. But most people know roughly what it means, and usually don't even try to give it its French pronunciation, which is itself a good sign that speakers of English accept it. In other words, *malaise* should have been naturalised long since. But it seems to have settled in limbo, and it seems unlikely it will ever emerge into the fully 'naturalised' light of day.

Then there are some words that have real difficulty getting their *meanings* into English. In these cases the word-forms themselves have had little difficulty, but the semantic content just cannot get a proper foothold. It is as if there were some cultural barrier which eventually screens out the new meaning, even though the need for the new concept is beyond dispute.

The word *gentil* 'high-born, noble' was borrowed from French during the Middle Ages, (at a time when hundreds of French words entered English) as *gentle*. Anglo-Saxon did have excellent words for 'noble', 'nobility', etc. but the French word ousted them and became the standard term. Although *gentle* survives as a very commonly used English word, its original meaning was lost, roughly at the same time as the modern meaning 'gentle in manner' became widespread; that is, about the middle of the sixteenth century. The English language, therefore, suddenly experiencing again a shortage of words to express 'well-born, noble, of good family', decided to borrow the French word *gentil* once more; this time as *genteel*. This second time round, the word preserved a degree of semblance to its (older) French pronunciation; at least the accent was not shifted on to the first syllable (as had happened with *gen'til* —→ *'gentle*). This was in Shakespeare's time. However, very soon, *genteel* could only be used in a sarcastic sense to describe high birth and nobility, no doubt as a result of the Civil Wars and the popular reaction against Monarch and Lords. After the Restoration, when Lords and Ladies had been returned to their proper places, in all their Louis XIV-style finery and extravagance, the English language had one final try. English borrowed *gentil* yet again, this time in its suitably anglicised Modern French pronunciation, as *jaunty*. It took no time at all, a matter of a mere ten years, for *jaunty* to acquire its modern meaning of 'sprightly in manner'. The tempting conclusion is that English has had no room for the concept embodied in the French word *gentil*, and had therefore no need to try to expunge its associations in a bloody revolution.

Words may not only be borrowed, but they can be returned to the language from which they originated. The English word *money* is derived from an Old French word meaning 'coinage' (and survives in Modern French *monnaie* = 'small change'). In recent times, during the height of French reborrowing from English ('Franglais'), in the 1950s and 60s, *monnaie* acquired the meaning of 'money in general'. A complex case is *typhoon*. The word *typhoon* may derive originally from Cantonese *daifung* ('strong wind', particularly of the violent kind familiar in the Western Pacific), though it is probably also influenced by the mythological Greek God *Typhon*, the stirrer up of tempests, as well as by Hindi *ṭūfān* 'hurricane'; no less than three different sources. In modern times, *typhoon* has been borrowed back into Cantonese as *taifung* 'typhoon' and exists alongside *daifung* which is merely a 'strong wind'.

Languages like English, which have a tendency towards unrestrained borrowing, will sometimes end up with more terms than it needs. We have already seen that exact synonyms, like *somnambulist* and *sleepwalker*, can go on existing happily side by side. More usually, however, words that have the same meaning and function in the same context tend to acquire divergent meanings. A very clear-cut case is *skirt* and *shirt*. These words are from Scandinavian and Old English (Anglo-Saxon) respectively, and both meant a knee-length garment. When the two words found themselves coexisting in late Old English and Middle English, the sex differentiation developed: *skirt* becoming in Modern English a female and *shirt* a male garment. During the later Middle Ages, following the Norman Conquest, when French and English were used by different classes of the English population, the English (i.e. Anglo-Saxon) speaker would continue to use words like *pig* or *sheep*, while a Norman (i.e. French) speaker would use *porc* and *mouton*, respectively. After a significant part of the English population had become bilingual, the words fell into the modern pairs of *pig-pork*, *sheep-mutton*, *bull-beef*, *deer-venison*, etc., the second member of the pair having the culinary sense. This was no doubt partly due to the fact that many Norman French speakers would only come into contact with the various animals at table, in the form of cooked meat.

Words that function in the same context — like *sleepwalker* and *sommambulist* — are assigned to different REGISTERS. *Sleepwalker* is the ordinary term used to describe someone who has the tendency to walk in his/her sleep, whereas *somnambulist* refers to a 'specialist' register, being appropriate mainly in medical contexts. Another type of register is that of DOMAIN. The words *audience*, *congregation* and *rally* all suggest a 'gathering', but *audience* has a theatrical connotation, while a *congregation* is usually found in a church or chapel, and *rally* often suggests sport or politics. A third type of register contrasts 'neutral' with 'pejorative' use. *Gathering* is neutral, but *mob* has sinister connotations. The existence of such a wealth of synonyms in English, largely the result of borrowing, has resulted in intricate arrays of register.

Take the case of *friend*. The word *friend* itself is neutral, whereas *companion* and *acquaintance*, both words deriving from Old French, contain a hint of reserve. *Mate* (from Low German), *pal*, *chum* and *crony* are used in more colloquial 'chummy' contexts. Both *chum* and *crony* derive from University slang, the latter being related to Greek *chronos* ('time'), while *pal* has its origin in an English Gypsy dialect. Though *mate* suggests the easy solidarity of everyday, the compound word *soul-mate* points to quite another extreme.

So far, our hasty survey of the lexical phenomenon of borrowing has presented us with some curious facets. But we are only likely to become really baffled by what goes on if we set up words as idols. Words are never more than a reflection of human culture, a particular human culture in its historical evolution. Word borrowing is obviously, then, one of the major ways in which cultures can potentially influence each other; although, as we have seen, borrowed words (or loan words) quickly adapt to the host culture, or if they don't adapt, they either get dropped or undergo radical changes of sense.

One phenomenon which has so far eluded precise description is that referred to as *semantic borrowing*. In the case of semantic borrowing no actual words are borrowed; only *meanings*. The question immediately arises: How can meanings, which are intangible entities, be 'borrowed' from one language to another? Well, an honest answer is that nobody really knows. All we do know for certain is that such semantic borrowing cannot occur outside a bilingual milieu: in other words, there must be speakers in significant stable numbers who speak the two languages between which borrowing takes place. This bilingual 'community' need not be very large or even very compact: a group of scholars or other specialists spread thinly over the globe is sufficient, provided they are somehow or other in frequent contact.

Nor need the two cultures, between which meanings are borrowed, be very close. The Greek language and culture was a vastly different one from the Hebrew, from which however the Greeks successfully absorbed many Mosaic and Christian, but otherwise alien, concepts. Concepts like *sin, righteous, angel, ungodly, idol, Paradise,* and hundreds of others were successfully transmitted via New Testament Greek to the whole of the Roman and Western world at the time of the rise of early Christianity. Sometimes these concepts found suitable verbal receptacles in Greek, sometimes not. The concept 'idol' itself, of Jewish origin, came to be associated with the Greek word *eidolon*, dating back to Democritus, having more to do with 'image' and 'imagination' than with idols proper. However the marriage of the Hebrew *concept* and the Greek *word* here led to a supra-concept which has stood us in good stead ever since. Over the centuries words acquire integral meanings built up of strands from a number of different traditions. Very often, when we identify a word as, say, characteristically English we may be justified, but in some instances the word will be an amalgam. Take, for example, *God*. This is a word whose form is English but whose semantics is drawn from Hebrew, Greek, Roman, old Germanic (Anglo-Saxon), with perhaps even a tinge of Celtic.

These 'invisible imports', or semantic borrowings, will tend to reflect widespread, and in modern times, world-wide concepts or techniques. Words like socialist, communist, bourgeois or capitalist may have their actual origins in French political radicalism, in the aftermath of the French Revolution, but only occasionally have the actual meanings themselves been borrowed exactly into the literary languages of the world. Sometimes a word in the host language will accommodate itself semantically. In English, the word *red*, along with the remainder of European languages, acquired the meaning 'Communistic, or extreme left-wing', from the French *rouge* ('red'), which had itself developed that particular meaning only a few years earlier.

Between American English and British English there has been a longish history of semantic borrowing, mainly in the direction American —> British. *Barbecue* once meant 'a rude framework for sleeping on'; *cocktail* was once a 'cock-tailed horse' or a 'lout', *liquor* was merely any liquid, but today the American meanings are the only ones familiar to us.

The strangest, if most widespread and predictable type of semantic borrowing, is what linguists have called *loan translation*. What happens is that a word concept develops in a particular language or culture, and from there spreads out to other languages until every language that has a need for the word finds itself with the requisite form (or forms). For example: *skyscraper* is a term coined in America in the 1890s. When other cities in other countries built or needed to refer to 'skyscrapers', they did not borrow the American word, but coined their own through loan translation. Thus, French, German and Russian have *gratte-ciel*, *Wolkenkratzer* and *neboskryob* respectively. *Peninsula*, a word borrowed centuries ago by English from Latin, meaning 'almost an island', has given *presqu'ile* 'almost an island' in French, but *Halbinsel*, *poluostrov* and *bundou* 'half an island' in German, Russian and Chinese (Cantonese), respectively. Other word-concepts have been only partially successful in finding loan translations. *Telephone* is one such. Many languages have simply borrowed the original word for this late nineteenth- century invention, sometimes modifying the spelling or form. German happens to have the direct loan translation *Fernsprecher* 'distance-speaker', but other languages contain adapted loan translations, such as for instance Chinese, which has 'electric speech'.

* * *

This brief and limited tour into the realm of word borrowing will perhaps provoke readers to make explorations of their own. And, as we have seen, there is no need to venture beyond English. Given a decent historical dictionary such as the Shorter Oxford and a modicum of interest, one can quickly lose oneself for a whole evening at a time in what must surely be one of the most curious and absorbing of all pastimes.

Notes and Suggested Further Reading

Word borrowing is covered in various of the works already referred to. A very comprehensive account of word borrowing in English is to be found in T. Pyles and J. Algeo: The Origins and Development of the English Language *(Chapter 12, 3rd Edn., New York, 1982) This can profitably be supplemented by a reading of the earlier chapters of Jespersen's* Growth and Structure of the English Language *(9th Edn., Oxford, 1967) A reading of C.S. Lewis:* Studies in Words *(Cambridge, 1961) and Owen Barfield's* History in English Words *(London, 1933) can be recommended at this stage.*

7

HOW ARE NEW WORDS CREATED?

One of the most difficult of tasks is to invent a new word. And hardest of all: to create a word which *bears no relation to existing words* and which other people will accept. It is no good coming up with new words like *blonk* or *stivering* or *plooze*, even if you provide a respectable dictionary meaning, as long as other people have no use for them. In fact, so few words of this sort have entered the English language that you could write them on one side of a postcard. Such etymology-less words are, for some reason, nearly always words with commercial currency, like *nylon*, *dacron*, *biro* or *zip*.

New word-forms nearly always consist of elements from, or are adaptations of, already existing words. Adaptations are by far the most common. But, before taking a look at these, we might mention just one class of neologism which is *not* the result of adaptation.

Here we are dealing with a highly productive means of word creation, which many people however find tiresome. I am referring to the *acronym*: a word consisting mainly or entirely of the initial letters of a phrase. Most acronyms remain proper nouns, and are commonly acronymous abbreviations of names of international organizations — UNESCO, for example — or public institutions, like BBC (British Broadcasting Corporation) or BM (for British Museum), or other, like *c.v.* for 'curriculum vitae'. One sub-class of acronyms, however, started life as a euphemistic device, to conceal words or phrases people did not want to hear. Among the earliest were WC (water closet), TB (tuberculosis), DTs (delirium tremens) and VD (venereal disease). Most members of this sub-class are medical terms, and have been most recently capped by that acronymous disease of all diseases — AIDS. Another sub-class consists of technical words, among the better known of which are *radar* (*ra*dio *d*etecting *a*nd *r*anging) and *laser* (*l*ight *a*mplification by *s*timulated *e*mission of *r*adiation).

Now for the *adaptations*, which occupy the remainder of this chapter.

Among the commonest methods of adaptation is *compounding*. Compounding is the running together, into a single word, of two or more existing words. All languages make use of compounding, some more than others. English is particularly rich in verbal compounds. In compound words the component parts (i.e. the original words) have undergone a certain amount of semantic change. The change may be slight, as in words like *windmill, babysitter*, or *high school*, where the meaning of the whole is 'transparent' and can be gathered approximately from the component words. Or the new meaning may be so different, so 'opaque', that it has completely superseded the separate meanings of the words that make it up. Examples of the latter are *disc-jockey, broadcast, will o' the wisp* and *ladybird*. Some compounds are so ancient that the fact that they were once compounds has been completely forgotten. In Anglo-Saxon, a *lord* was a *hláfweard* 'a loaf-keeper' and his *lady* a *hla-dige* or 'loaf kneader'. A *hussy* was a later reduction of '*housewife*'. Chaucer was not fantasising when he wrote 'The *dayesye*, or elles the ye of the day' since that is exactly what the *daisy* was: 'the eye of the day'. The full pronunciation of the sign *&* is *ampersand*: not that ancient, but how many readers know that this word started life as 'and per se and'? We shall be taking a further look at word compounding in a later chapter.

Another method of adaptation is *affixation*. In English, an affix is either a *prefix*— an element occuring at the beginning of a word — or a *suffix*, which occurs at the end. The most highly productive are affixes borrowed from Latin or Greek. Once these affixes enter English they take on a semantic life of their own. The suffix -*ese* for example, came into English from French in medieval times, but in current usage this suffix has taken on a peculiar slant. We now have words like *journalese*, *officialese*, and even *computerese*. The implication here is a spuriousness of communication or expression.

The prefix *de-* and the suffix -*ise*, often used in conjunction, as for example in *demoralise*, *deregionalise*, or *depersonalise*, received their scathing due from writers like George Orwell, who warned against the insidious ease with which such 'prefabricated' terms could be assembled: once in the language they are very difficult to get rid of, if only because they are so convenient to use, despite their studied woolliness.

Affixes not directly from Greek or Latin include -*wise*, *mini-* and -*nik*. The element -*wise* has been in the language for a very long time, as in *clockwise* or *likewise*, but it was only after the Second World War that this suffix came into its own. We suddenly found ourselves with a host of new terms, from *sales-wise*, *weather-wise*, *investment-wise* to *personality-wise* and *incometax-wise*. We have to do here, one suspects, with rather more than a suffix, and with something approaching an adverb. The suffix -*nik* from Yiddish, reinforced by Russian *sputnik* in the 1950s, has produced *beatnik*, *no-goodnik* and, more recently, *refusednik* 'a person who is refused an exit visa from the Soviet Union'. *Mini-* appears to be a shortened version of *miniature* and *minimum*. Since the 1960s *mini* has become a widely used suffix. Among recent current uses are *minicab*, *mini-lecture*, *mini-edition*, *mini-thesis*, *mini-computer* and a host of others.

An intricate kind of compounding occurs when two (or more) different words are mixed together, rather like shuffling a pack of cards. The practice is well-established in English. Older examples include: *twirl* which is a mixture of *twist* and *whirl*; *flurry*, a knocking together of *flutter* and *hurry*; and *flush* which could well be a mixture of as many as three different forms: *gush*, *flash* and *blush*. Lewis Carroll was a particular exponent of this type of word blending, and he called the results 'portmanteau' words. Two of his creations have now a permanent place in English: they are

52

chortle, which blends *chuckle* and *snort*, and *galumph*, a mixture of *gallop* and *triumph*. Modern English has spawned many such blends, less out of poetic impulsion than utilitarian convenience. *Smog* ('smoke fog'), *motel* ('motor hotel'), *brunch* ('breakfast and lunch'), *motorcade* ('motor cavalcade'), *workaholic* ('work' plus 'alcoholic'), and many hundred of others, some quite funny, as in *palimony* 'financial support of unmarried ex-partner', others politically loaded, as in *Irangate*, still others neutral and mnemonically quite useful, for example *quasar* ('quasi-stellar object'). A few fall into the category of folk etymology, touched upon earlier. Good examples of this are *beefburger*, *cheeseburger* and many other 'burgers', which are coined on the misunderstanding that a *hamburger* is 'ham' plus 'burger', instead of 'something associated with the city of Hamburg'. (I can't be the only one to have been told by a waitress: 'We don't have hamburgers, only beefburgers, or cheeseburgers'.)

A type of word formation which combines popular etymology with legitimate processes of English lexical morphology has come to be known as *back formation*. What happens in back formations is that a new word is created by false analogy, and subsequently continues to be used as if it were a true (i.e. historically derived) form. In Middle and Early Modern English it was not difficult for speakers, especially the vast majority of illiterate speakers, to hear a final *-s* as an indication of plural when the noun was in fact singular. This was the case with *pea* which started out as *pease*; and *cherry* which began life as *cherise*, after being borrowed from Old French, but in a comparatively short time had become reduced to *cheri(e)* in English.

The practice of back formation is by now well-established, and useful. Until the last century there never was a verb *to burgle*, though there was a *burglar*, nor anyone to *buttle*, though *butler* has been around for some time. Shakespeare gave us the richly loaded verb *grovel*, even though *grovelling* from which the word *grovel* derives is etymologically descended from a noun *gruf(e)-ling* 'someone lying with his face downwards'. Today we use a fair number of back formations without realising that they are such. Unselfconsciously, we use verbs like *baby-sit*, *type* (from *typewriter*), *breast-feed*, *locomote*, and many more besides.

53

There are still other ways in which existing words can be turned into new words but, since space is running out, I will deal with only two.

One of these ways is hugely interesting and rather more complex than one might at first suspect. It has to do with the transformation of proper names into common nouns, and the derivation of words from personal or place names.

A tiny group of verbs derived from people's names are not only well-established, but it is also difficult to be sure why these words are so few and what are the restrictions on more being created. I am thinking of words like *boycott* (from the 19th century captain of that name), *lynch* (after a somewhat earlier American captain), *pander* and *hector* (both from classical literature).

Other words are derived from the names of their inventors or creators. Words like *zeppelin, volt, watt, macintosh, derrick* (originally the surname of a Tyburn hangman, only later applied to a hoisting contrivance), and several more.

For me, the most intriguing of all are what might be called the 'mythological' group — or rather, groups. The first group relates to the classical (pagan) mythology: *mercury, mercurial, saturnine, nemesis,* or to the classical world more generally: *stoical, epicure, platonic, laconic, spartan,* etc. Curiously parallel to the latter are the biblically derived terms which, unlike their Greek counterparts, more often have negative connotations: *jeremiah, babel, sodomy, maudlin* (from Magdalen), *philistine,* and so forth.

Three words which call for special comment however are *panic, psyche* (along with their derivatives *psychic,* and *psychology*), and *erotic.* None of the three was in English until the 17th century, and most of their semantic development occurred previous to that time in other European languages. Yet they fill important gaps in our language. There is no ready substitute, for example, for *panic,* which derives from the nature god Pan ('all'), and suggests contagious running amuck. *Psyche* probably needs no further comment. *Erotic* fills a gap in our post-Romantic vocabulary, especially when we want a term which does not foreground the affectionate, friendshiplike, charitable connotations of love, and at the same time want to avoid 'sexual' as an adjective paired with 'love'.

The second 'mythological' group is what I am tempted to call *makeshift* mythology. It consists mainly of three words, with their compounds: *tom, bill, jack*. *Tom* has overtones of socially (rather than morally) reprehensible behaviour, as in *tomboy, tommyrot, tomfool* and *tomcat*. *Billy* sometimes suggests lack of sophistication, as in *hillbilly*, or *silly billy*, but not when used of machines. *Jack* sometimes indicates contempt, as in *jackass, jack-of-all-trades* or *cheapjack*, but not however in *lumberjack* or *jack-in-the-box*. *John* and *Johnny* also have currency, but mainly in American English. (The use in British English of *johnny* as a term of contempt really belongs to colloquialism).

The last group of word creations we shall be considering are *shortened* words. Shortening or clipping can occur at the beginning or end of a word. *Bus, taxi, pants, pram, mob* (short for *mobile vulgus* 'the fickle common people') *bra, zoo, advert* (and more recently, *ad*) *high tech, perk* (from *perquisite*) *hype, pop* are all examples of words that have lost a substantial part of their original form. With some of them, as in the case of *mob* or *perk*, the 'full' forms are unknown, or known only to relatively few. In other cases the clipping may be from the start of the word, like *(tele)phone* or *(a)cute*, or *(de)fender*, or *ticket* (from *etiquette*). A word like *flu* is the result of clipping from both the beginning and end of the word, the full form being, of course, *influenza*.

* * *

Too soon, then, we take leave of this endlessly fascinating domain of word creation. A historically based dictionary such as The *Shorter Oxford English Dictionary* or, if you have access to it, the many-volumed *Oxford English Dictionary*, now available in a single volume, with magnifying glass, as well as for use on CD-ROM, will provide a host of other examples of words falling within the categories we have outlined, together with numerous others. For contemporary usage, there is no substitute for the notebook which, if well kept, will record a surprising number of new and deviant uses of words.

Notes and Suggested Further Reading

A reading of Chapter 11 of Pyles and Algeo (see above, Notes, etc. to Chapter 6, for reference) would be appropriate at this stage. Many of the longer works previously referred to will have touched on the creation of new words. You could also refer to Ross: Etymology, *(London, 1958) and have another look at Bolinger and Sears (for reference see above), Chapter 10.*

8

WORDS AS STRUCTURES

So far we have explored some of the ways in which words are used: how they may have originated, how they change their meanings, and how new words come into being. But we have said very little about the composition of words as such.

The use of the term 'structures' in the title of this chapter suggests that words do have structures, in the same way perhaps that buildings have architectural structures, or animal bodies anatomical structures. That is correct, in the sense that many words in a language do exhibit structures whether of the architectural or the anatomical kind.

The 'architectural' analogy is the easiest. In English, *unkindness* consists of three units — *un*, *kind* and *ness* — which are combined into a single word which we call a noun. Indeed, the suffix -*ness* in English is invariably a sign of noun derivation, an indication that another word-form (in this case the adjective *unkind*) has been transformed into a noun. Here we have taken three units of language and assembled them into a structure. *Kind* appears to be somehow more important than *un* or *ness*, as it is supported by both of the latter; in a remotely comparable way perhaps to the way in which pillars support a beam. Many similar structures can

57

be found in other European languages. In German we find words like *Menschlichkeit* 'humaneness', again made up of three units *Mensch* 'man, human', *lich* (English *-ly*) and *keit* '-ness'. The now popular word in Russian — *glasnost'* 'openness' — contains a form *glasn-*, meaning 'public, open', and *-ost'* which is the exact equivalent of English *-ness*.

At other times, the architectural analogy does not take us very far. We need a more 'organic' model, of the kind anatomists rely upon. Here the separate units depend upon one another, not only in the way that a beam is supported by a pillar, but to the extent that the different units are organically interdependent. The heart depends on the lungs, liver and other organs of the body, and all in turn depend on the brain; just as the brain in its turn depends on them for its oxygen supply and other nutrients. If we take an adjective like *strong* and convert it into a noun, we not only add a suffix *-th*, but at the same time we have to do something which completely transforms *strong* into *streng-*, giving us *strength*.

The organic analogy applies even more powerfully if we consider some further examples. The English words *sun* and *moon* can be converted into adjectival forms such as *sunny* and *moony*, but for their principal adjectival forms we have to look to *solar* and *lunar*. Here the 'roots' *sol-* and *lun-* bear no immediate relation to *sun* or *moon*; and unless we know some Latin, or some basic etymology, we shall not be aware of any connection. This happens quite frequently in English where Latin has played such an important role. Consider, for example, what has happened in the following sample:

[*leg-*] —> *legible* —> *legibility*. *Read* —> *readable* —> *readability*

In this instance we have the verb *read* and the (non-occurring) Latin verb root **leg-* and their respective adjectival and noun (nominal) derivations. There is nothing unusual about the Anglo-Saxon word-form *read* acquiring an Old French suffix *-able* to make an adjective, or a Latinate suffix *-ability* to form a noun. The interesting thing is the parallelism, in both meaning and form, with (**leg-*) —> *legible* —> *legibility*. The meaning of *legible* is close to *readable*, and the two are interchangeable in some everyday contexts, but if we are to apply stricter norms, we shall use *legible* only to highlight the quality of handwriting or print (*His handwriting is quite legible*, but *The article he has written is not very readable*).

On rare occasions the connection between the noun and its adjective are known only to the etymologist. How many people are aware of the etymological connection between *thing* 'an entity of any kind' and *real*? *Thing* happens to be a perfectly good Anglo-Saxon word. But for some reason it has no derived adjectival forms. We have of course *thing-like*, but not **thingly*, which would have been perfectly possible. Instead, in the late Middle Ages the form *real* was borrowed (ultimately) from Latin: *re-* being the thing and *-al* the suffix we are familiar with in many other English words. Nowadays, the semantic distance between *thing* and *real* is so great that we make no natural connection between them whatsoever. Furthermore, even the verb *realize* (formerly 'to make real') has also lost its semantic link with *real*. (The philosophical term *reify* is not in direct line, referring as it does to the Latin word for 'thing' (*res*), rather than to English *thing*).

It is at this point, therefore, that we are obliged to ponder whether there can be any order behind all this seeming chaos.

A solution to our dilemma may be found in an *abstract* entity which underlies any cluster of different word-forms which are obviously related in meaning and grammatical function. This is the *lexeme*, by now a well-established concept in linguistics. The lexeme has been defined as the fundamental unit of the lexicon, which underlies all the different variants (word-forms) which occur within a single word class. Thus, *bring, brings, bringing, brought* all represent the verb lexeme BRING. Note however that *bring* is simply the dictionary citation-form of what is really an abstract BRING, which could be just as well represented by *bringing, brings* and *brought* as by *bring*. Likewise *man* and *men* can be said to be different word-forms of lexeme MAN.

There is nothing mysterious about the lexeme as such. In most cases the lexeme is satisfactorily represented by the citation-forms listed in the dictionary. It has the advantage, however, of explaining why equivalent word-forms should in some instances be identified as *homonyms* (words spelt and/or pronounced the same but differing in meaning). For example, the homonymous, *lying*[1] ('being in a recumbent position') and *lying*[2] ('speaking falsely') can be assigned to the different lexemes LIE[1] and LIE[2].

The lexeme, as a concept, though, is less useful when we want it to work for us. As we saw, *lying* could be identified as a possible member of two lexemes LIE[1] and LIE[2]. But what about *readable*? Does that belong to a different lexeme from READ, or is it like *lying*, just another word-form member of LIE[1] or LIE[2]? According to the dictionary, *readable* is a separate entry from *read*. But so too is *lying*, and, if *readable* is a form of lexeme *READ*, what about *legible*? Is that a form of lexeme *LEG* (LEG[2] presumably, to distinguish it from LEG[1], the body part, or LEG[3] 'to walk fast')? The dictionary is unhelpful since it does not list anything that can be identified as LEG[2]. Presumably, the dictionary compilers are of the opinion that LEG[2] is merely a root, and many of those who consult the dictionary would concur.

The logic is all in place. The difficulty — Where does one draw the line? — is really a question of practical convenience and consistency. Even if the lexeme proves to be something more than just another 'ghost in the machine', it will remain an elusive entity. And when it comes to more outlandish problems, like the possible relationship between the *re-* of *real* and *thing*, the concept lexeme will not help us one bit. Similarly, it will remain neutral in debates about, say, whether *culinary* is lexically related to *cook*. Resolving an issue like the latter will very much depend on your etymological awareness of the link between the two words, and possibly even a basic knowledge of Latin. Again, if you want to insist that *pneumatic* must be assigned to two lexemes: PNEUMATIC[1] ('having to do with air or breath') and PNEUMATIC[2] ('spiritual'), the dictionary (OED) will not support you. On the other hand, the ordinary speaker of English may be familiar only with sense number one — as in 'pneumatic tyre' or 'pneumatic drill' — and may feel, on encountering pneumatic in the second sense, that this is a different 'word' somehow. Only the speaker who knows that both meanings have to do with the conceptually complex Greek word *pneuma* will be happy with what the dictionary has to say. But even he (or she) would probably jib, on hearing someone say: 'Yoga is really a kind of pneumatic drill'(!)

We are brought back then to where we started. In Chapter 1,

the claim was made that the word is a 'piece of culture'. This in turn, if true, implies that a word is a kind of socio-cultural institution; not something fixed for all time, but subject to change as the society or culture that support it change.

This claim can be further illustrated, and to some extent supported, by taking a look at the knotty problem of *derivation* in English.

Linguistics, ever since ancient times, has claimed that the grammar of language is rule-governed. Modern linguistics has come up with even stronger claims. Chomsky, and those associated with his theory of language, have argued that linguistics is really a branch of psychology, and have implied that language structure, or *grammar*, gives us direct insight into the structure and function of the human brain and nervous system.

Grammar cannot however function in the abstract like algebra. There has to be flesh on the bones. And the flesh is provided by the lexicon. As such the lexicon, words, interact with the grammar (Chomsky has gone further and insisted that they are an integral part of it) at all points. Word-forms, for example, are made up of sequences of sounds (phonemes) governed by very precisely understood phonological rules and processes. Purely functional parts of words, like inflexional endings, such as plurals, genders, cases, etc., also fit fairly tightly into a rule-governed system. Thus, in English, if you want the plural of the noun *cat*, you have to say *cats*, *dog* has to become *dogs*, etc. Whether you pronounced a final [z] or an [s] is again governed by precise rules we need not go into. There is a small hard core, nevertheless, of quite commonly used nouns that do not follow the rules. If you want the plural of *man*, you have to say *men*, for *tooth* you have say *teeth*. In the case of *sheep*, nothing is added or changed. *Ox* takes the plural form *oxen*, and *child* becomes *children*. Furthermore, English at one period in its history acquired the odd habit of using Latin and Greek, and even Hebrew, plurals for some types of noun borrowed from these languages. We have *phenomenon* and its plural *phenomena*, *focus* and *foci* (although the dictionary does permit *focuses*). How many people use the official plural *stigmata* for *stigma* (in place of *stigmas*)? And then, with a noun like *syllabus*, we are stumped: some say *syllabuses* while others insist on *syllabi*. The dictionary informs us that the word *syllabus* is spurious anyway, the result of faulty late Renaissance transcription. In that case *syllabi* can only be correct by analogy. And, lastly, what about compound nouns, such as *mother-in-law*, *man-of-war*, *attorney general*, which do not follow the rule of adding the plural *-s* to the *end* of the word? In fact you *can* use (though probably not *write*) final *-s* and get away with it. But, whatever you may say, the official plurals remain *mothers-in-law*, *men-of-war*, and *attorneys general*. Those who object that really we are dealing with optional alternatives (like *syllabuses* or *syllabi*), and that speakers never make the mistake of double pluralising, as in *mothers-in-laws or *men-of-wars, may be given pause for thought by the (official) double plural of *gentleman farmer*: *gentlemEn farmerS*.

The plural inflexions in English already make plain the tension between a rule-governed tendency on the one hand and an institutionalising tendency on the other; as if the two tendencies are holding one another in check. Institutionalism will be found to be most common among the oldest and best- established word-forms in the language. Predictions, on the other hand, about the plurals of more recent forms, or forms borrowed from contemporary languages, will nearly always be proved correct. This situation is best illustrated for that class of noun for which there sometimes exist different female forms. If in doubt, a speaker can for human female animate beings always prefix *female*, *woman*, (or *lady* for the more traditional) to the male noun, whether it be *doctor*, *driver*, *pilot*, *teacher* (as in *woman doctor*, *lady driver*, *female pilot*, etc.) But some of these forms do have 'official' female forms: e.g. *heir-heiress*, *god-goddess*, *conductor*(of a bus)-*conductress*, *actor-actress*, *marquis-marchioness* and many others. With animals, again one can prefix *she-* or *female*, though the standard female forms are more various: *sheep-ewe*, *stallion-mare*, *bull-cow*, *pig-sow*, *fox-vixen*, *peacock-peahen* etc., but *female hippopotamus*, *she-wolf*, *female jaguar*, *female shark*, *she-cat* (though in this case there does exist a specific *male* form: *tomcat*). The choice of *female* or *she-* would take us into a different problem, of the sort not uncommon in English. There must obviously be rules, even if no one really knows what they are. (The existence of this curious phenomenon led the genial American linguist-anthropologist Whorf to argue for the existence of what he called 'covert categories': nothing shows up on the surface of these nouns, but they must somehow contain information that determines what their gender is.)

With nouns containing derivations (Lyons has called them 'complex lexemes') institutionalism is even more prevalent. Although certain derivational affixes may be semantically predictable up to a point, the range of predictability is usually not too great. Let us take -*able* as our first example. As we saw earlier, -*able* is a borrowing from Late Medieval French, and ultimately from medieval Latin. We have many forms in which we know -*able* means 'capable of being'. Thus *readable* does indeed mean 'capable of being read', *singable* 'capable of being sung', *translatable* 'capable of being translated', *obtainable* 'capable of being obtained', and so on. But as we press on, we may find ourselves in a grey area. *Likeable* if paraphrased as 'capable of being liked' may give us some unease. This is really because it is an adjective coined to introduce a grade of difference between it and lovable, which is semantically quite regular ('capable of being loved'). Finally, we move into a semantically anomalous region, with derived lexemes like *payable*, not *'capable of being paid', but 'falling due for payment'; *knowledgeable*, 'having a wide range of knowledge'; *reasonable* (more than two different meanings, but not including *'capable of being reasoned'); or several others. Then, there is the sometimes equally puzzling existence of the two derivations -*able* and -*ible*. The latter frequently means 'capable of being', but is more often associated with roots which are not free-standing lexemes. Latin has provided a fair number of such roots. One such is *ed*-, yielding *edible*, 'capable of being eaten'; another would be *leg*- (*legible* 'capable of being read'), a third *intellig*- (*intelligible* 'capable of being understood'), and so forth. But note that in some cases these forms in -*ible* contrast with other forms in -*able*. As we saw earlier, *readable* and *legible* have different but related meanings, the latter being more specialised in meaning, having to do with handwriting or print. *Eatable* is not quite the same in meaning as *edible*. *Eatable* implies that food is decently prepared, whereas *edible* has no such implication. Thus it is possible in English to say: *The meal was just about edible but not what you could call eatable*. Also, users of English are not always clear about which derivation to use. *Feasible* may turn up as **feasable*, and *commendable* and **commendible*.

Another common derivational affix in nouns is *-al*. Nouns like *refusal, approval, appraisal, trial* and *recital* are derived from verbs by using this affix. *Approval* always entails the same meaning as that of the verb *approve* from which it is derived. Likewise, *appraisal* and *appraise* are similarly related, as well as scores of others (e.g. *arouse-arousal, carouse-carousal, refer-referral*, etc.). However, the reader may already have noticed that the semantics of a particular derivation is not that simple. *Trial* is regular when it means 'the action of testing or trying out', but not when it takes on its everyday meaning as in *He's something of a trial*. *Recital* does not always entail *recite*, though it sometimes does (as in *the recital of his misdeeds*.) As Lyons has said, 'What constitutes and is referred to in English as a recital is determined by accepted cultural conventions, and one cannot be said to know the meaning of 'recital' unless one has some knowledge of these conventions'.

*   *   *

What at the outset promised to be a fairly straightforward undertaking has turned out to be something of monstrous complexity.

It seems as if there are two opposing principles at work in language. One of these we can call *grammar*, whether in the more traditional, Chomskyan, or post-Chomskyan, or other sense. The other is the *lexicon* itself. The lexicon behaves according to its own lights, at times as if the rules of syntax and of inflexional and derivational morphology counted for little, or even nothing. Indeed, it has been said that the lexicon secretes its own grammar: each word (? lexeme) appears to be, as it were, surrounded by its own grammatical halo. Extrapolating along the lines of such a theory, it could even be suggested that what we know as grammar may be no more than the secretion, the geological deposit, of continuous and dynamic lexical activity. English, one might argue, has clear-cut word classes of noun and adjective and clear-cut delineation between verb and preposition, because over the centuries and millennia this is what the lexicon has laid down, deposited, as it were. In Chinese on the other hand, the boundaries are far less clear-cut, again because the Chinese lexicon has developed differently.

This may be a speculative note to end on. But such a line of enquiry is not so impossible now that we have large data bases, including the entire Oxford English Dictionary, available to the computer user.

Notes and Suggested Further Reading

A very comprehensive work to read at this time is P.H. Matthews: Morphology: An Introduction to the Theory of Word Structure *(Cambridge, 1974). This can be supplemented by J. Lyons:* Semantics *(Cambridge, 1977), Chapter 13. For a readable short account see Akmajian, Demers, and Harnish (reference given above), Chapter 5. A comprehensive recent study is that by D.A. Cruse (*Lexical Semantics, *Cambridge, 1986).*

9

HOW DO WE LEARN

TO USE WORDS?

Since the 1960s, much has become known about how human beings learn language. In the first place, we know that learning our mother tongue is not such a straightforward affair as was once thought. This is partly because language itself has been found to be an abstract hierarchy of function and structure, much of it very remote from the practical business of speaking; and partly because the learning of the mother tongue follows a biological programme. Small children do not simply learn their mother tongue piece by piece, but each 'piece' has to be acquired in relation to every other piece in accordance with a quite dazzling array of sequencing and rules. Until the necessary pieces are in place, nothing further can be mastered by the infant learner. Children may sometimes *appear* to learn by imitation or mimicry, but no amount of drilling by the parent will ensure proper acquisition until the child is biologically ready. Forcing a child to repeat segments of language for which he or she is not yet ready may actually promote slow learning.

For example, we know that learning even the sounds — the phonology of the language — which many would suppose to be the easiest phase of all, presents huge problems, since each phonological element (speech sounds: consonants, vowels, etc.) consists of a bundle of component parts. Every sound in the language consists of a particular limited selection of these component parts, rather like a Lego set which can be used for building different shapes and structures. The phonologists call these components 'distinctive features'. In crude terms — to take a simplified instance — sound [b] in English differs from sound [m] because it is not 'nasalised': that is, the sound does not travel through the nasal passage, but through the mouth. The same sound [b] differs from [p] because it requires the vocal cords, situated at the end of the windpipe, to be vibrating in a certain way (while [p] suppresses any such vibration). This phenomenon is known as 'voicing'. In English the sounds [m], [n] and [ng] share the component 'nasalisation'; while [b], [d], [g] and a number of other sounds share the feature of 'voicing'. These are but two components. Experts differ as to how many components exactly are built into a single sound, but it can be many.

My son Christopher was a good mimic at the age of six months, with the ability to pronounce complicated names like Caroline, quite distinctly. From about eight months onwards he went through a silent period, during which sequences like Caroline had obviously become too difficult, owing no doubt to his growing 'phonological' awareness. His speech only reemerged gradually with quite elementary babbling expressions like *em* or *mem* or *ba* (*ma-ma* appeared only round about 14 months). Even at 16 months (at the time when this Chapter was written), Christopher would not want to attempt a word like *Caroline*, or even *piano* which he could manage quite well at six months.

Nevertheless, although our knowledge of children's acquisition of language has been going from strength to strength, we still understand comparatively little about how a child learns *words*. Studies of verbal learning have tended to be carried out by psychologists rather than linguists, and, although as we shall see, this has not always been a limiting factor, most psychological studies have placed heavy reliance on word associations and countability. As far as linguistics is concerned, what I wrote more than ten years ago still holds good: that the vocabulary of the language goes on being treated as a cinderella, whereas, in fact, every other aspect of language learning is dwarfed by an amazing proliferation of word-forms, by the even vaster proliferation of different meanings and shades of meaning in their tens of thousands, and by the seemingly infinite shifts in meaning brought about by minute variations in context. (More on this in the next chapter).

One thing upon which most linguists would agree is that the word is not an integral all-or-nothing phenomenon; it is composite. A word may be composite in a variety of ways.

1. It will usually have a number of different *meanings*. For example, *bank* means (a) an institution for handling financial transactions, and (b) the shore-line of a river. *Head* can mean the topmost or foremost part of a body or the top person in an institution or department.

2. A word is often *formally* composite. It may be a compound. Quite often it will consist of affixes in addition to the main 'stem'. In many languages it may, in addition, have declensional endings.

In our last chapter we took a brief look at some of these formal complexities. The semantic level, however, — the level of meaning — has been even more controversial, and debate has centred around what the semantic constituents of a word actually are.

Part of the difficulty is that word meaning has at least two aspects, and these aspects are not obviously related. The first of these aspects has had a fairly high profile in modern linguistics. Briefly, it has to do with the coming together of abstract semantic 'components' or 'categories' out of which our perceived cosmos is built up. Componential analysis, which attempts to reduce a word to its component semantic 'primitives', has had a thriving career since the 1960s. The main problem is that there is wide disagreement as to what these semantic 'primitives' are. Sometimes the solutions themselves have been too 'primitive'. *Man, woman, boy* and *girl*, for example, have been analysed into semantic distinctive features, and so too have animal pairs:

	Human	Male	Adult
Man	+	+	+
Woman	+	-	+
Boy	+	+	-
Girl	+	-	-
Mare	-	-	+
Stallion	-	+	+

Sexist bias apart, such analyses clearly will not take us very far. Sometimes, solutions have been more elegant, if still highly limited in scope, as in the work of Bernard Pottier, where he shows how out of the following components:

(1) with legs
(2) for sitting upon
(3) with a back
(4) with arms

the French words *fauteuil* ('armchair'), *chaise* ('chair'), *canapé* ('sofa') and *tabouret* ('stool') can be distinguished from one another. *Fauteuil* has all four features; *chaise* does not have (4); *tabouret* has neither (3) nor (4). Other linguists have produced different models. In the 1960s, for example, the American linguists Katz and Fodor, proposed an analysis of *bachelor* illustrated by the 'tree-diagram' on the next page.

The items in the curved brackets were called semantic 'markers', and those in the square brackets 'distinguishers' or remainders. At first it looked as if the 'markers' were the 'primitives' that linguists had been looking for. But, later, these markers were found to be complex, with an internal structure all of their own, and capable of showing up as components of other semantic markers. Like every other semantic analysis to date it suffers from arbitrariness. For this and other reasons we cannot go into, the early promise of this model has not been fulfilled. At a far extreme from this, the Polish linguist Anna Wierzbicka has been maintaining that there are no more than 13 primitives for all languages, and that all statements can be reduced to a selection of these thirteen.

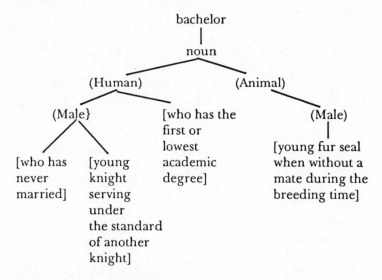

bachelor
|
noun

(Human)   (Animal)

(Male}   [who has the first or lowest academic degree]   (Male)

[who has never married]   [young knight serving under the standard of another knight]   [young fur seal when without a mate during the breeding time]

The second aspect has to do with the cultural content of a word, about which we know very little, scientifically speaking. The more distinctively cultural a word is perceived to be, the more subjective our investigations are likely to become. Peculiarly (British) English words like *home, countryside, seaside, picnic, hiking,* and many others, will certainly fall into this category. But even the fine shade of cultural difference between French *fauteuil* and English *armchair* will create equally thorny problems, including the possibility (following Wierzbicka and others) that there may not be any significant difference at all; or rather, the difference, if there is any, may not inhere within the structure of the vocabulary, or in the word itself, but in the cultural and psychological associations the word has acquired in use.

As we saw in our last chapter, words can usually be broken down into constituent parts. Sometimes, it does not require any particular sophistication to do this. A word like *player* obviously consists of *play* + *er*. We call these parts morphemes (and in this case the first constituent is also a lexeme). With other words, however, with longer Latinisms for example, we may find difficulty. A word like *pliability* consists of *ply* + *able* + *ity*. And a few words seem really problematic. Take the word *nothing*. Is this reducible to *no* + *thing*? This solution seems doubtful, to say the least. But with a whole host of words, like *courage, intent, larder*, or *summer*, for example, we are never in any doubt. These words simply cannot be subdivided. *Larder* is not a word like *player* where we can see, quite simply, that we have two elements: (1) 'someone' who (2) 'plays' (a *larder* is not someone who 'lards'.)

This kind of approach was first challenged in the 1950s by a French scholar, Guiraud. He showed that words of every kind can be subdivided. The parts into which words can be subdivided he showed may be many, and do not necessarily always correspond to accepted morphological subdivisions. Moreover, these subdivisions can and do have meaning.

Subsequently, this concept was taken up by the present author, who found, first in English and much later in Chinese, that these subdivisions are arranged hierarchically in systems, and that these subdivisions represent a complex array of 'morphosemantic' categories (the word 'morphosemantic', implying an indivisible bond of sound and meaning, is borrowed from Guiraud). The approach seems not to be particularly new, however, since it appears that Chinese linguists have been pursuing studies in this area for many centuries past.

In English and in Chinese (Cantonese), it has been shown, and empirically demonstrated, that these morphosemantic categories are not just figments of the imagination. Basically, it has been found that a word consists of an initial element and a final element. In single syllable words, of which there are many in Chinese, these elements overlap (in a word like *sam*, for example, we would find *sa* + *am*).

The basic morphosemantic element constitutes a real interface between form and meaning, at a level below the word. Unlike words, these morphosemantic elements do not have 'full' meanings; indeed, they cannot have by their very nature. But even though they do not have explicit denotation or full meaning, they appear none the less to be functions both of linguistic reality and, of social and cognitive reality. Also these elements are not something hard or rigid, like building bricks, but have 'elastic' boundaries, so to speak.

In English, the final elements appear to be the active ones, whereas the initial elements reflect more archaic layers of cultural history. These elements are quanta, but as we have said, they overlap at the formal level. For example, the English word TUNNEL can be subdivided as follows:

TUN(N) - EL

TU-(N)NEL

T-UNNEL

(1) the terminal segment -UNNEL is the most highly differentiated, not only in form but also in meaning. But it occurs only rarely, for example in *runnel*, which came to mean eventually a 'gutter', and which is often a kind of half cylinder, along which water runs. *Funnel* is also of interest. It suggests constriction rather than shape, but it is also cylindrical, like *tunnel*, at its tapered end.

(2) -*NEL* is less differentiated at the level of form, but brings together a much wider range of words. *Channel* and *runnel* share the same terminal morphosemantic element; whereas *panel* (in one of its more technical senses) and *cannel* are coalmining terms (*panel* denotes a piece of coal left uncut in a mine, *cannel* something between coal and shale which splits into parallel layers, like slate), though *panel* itself, in more general use, suggests flat layers, like *cannel*. *Flannel* and *cannel* are both names for pieces of cloth. *Gunwale* (pronounced, and sometimes spelt, *gunnel*), one of whose meanings is 'planking on the uppermost part of a ship', no doubt ties in with another meaning of *panel* 'a flat square piece of timber'.

(3) -*EL* on the other hand is so highly *un*differentiated that it cannot be said to have a unified cluster of meanings: it can identify a common element between a range of words like *swivel*, *handle*, *panel*, *trowel*, but it also occurs in hundreds of other words.

(4) *TUN*-, an initial element, suggests something fat and round, like a tun 'a large cask or barrel' which was an old word, probably Celtic, when it was borrowed into Medieval Latin (and thence into

English). The *tun* of *tunny*, the name for the massive tun-like fish or tuna, goes back to Indo-European.

At the abstract pinnacle of the morphosemantic system, there have emerged semantic categories like 'state, condition', 'change of state', 'action', 'orientation towards others', 'motion', 'space', 'time', 'quantity', 'quality'. Thus, we have a hierarchy of semantic categories and sub-categories, realised as particular morphosemantic elements.

This somewhat technical digression brings us back to our starting point.

It is a fact that we can only seldom consciously recall learning the particular words that we 'know'. We can of course remember looking up dictionaries, but how often have we remembered what we found there? How many of us can produce even partly reliable dictionary definitions of the meanings of the words we actually use? The argument that 'a vocabulary which is within the competence of the ordinary speaker is in the form in which the dictionary presents it' does not stand up to even the mildest of tests. The 'ordinary speaker' is notoriously incapable of producing anything like dictionary definitions. And even the 'sophisticated' speaker can frequently be upset to discover just how inaccurate his definitional knowledge of a particular dictionary item can be.

Whatever view we take, words are not often learnt as isolated dictionary-like entities, but their meanings are more usually acquired from a hierarchy of morphosemantic components and/ or semantic categories. Our neural synapses are no doubt arranged in such a way that the acquisition of vocabulary proceeds in a hierarchy-like manner. We can only be said to have 'learnt' a word after our brains have laid down the necessary formal and semantic pathways for them to be retained and retrieved as needed. From this it would follow that the lexicon in the individual is not a static thing, but something always in flux. We do not simply learn batteries of words, but a *system*. And it is this system, whatever its ultimate nature, which affords us the necessary capacity to produce an appropriate series of words once a situation calls for them. Often we will be somewhat wide of the mark, particularly in speech, where time does not allow a full search of our lexical memories. In general, no serious problem arises, because speech communication is also negotiation. Always we adapt to feedback. If we were to keep to what the dictionary prescribes, we would never get beyond the slowest and most wooden of interchanges; without humour, without conceit, without deviousness, without irony — what a bore it would all be!

What I was able to notice about young Christopher is that his first syllables did not denote anything or anybody, but were used in a wide variety of ways, expressively sometimes, on other occasions because he just wanted something. At other times, he seemed happy just with the sounds, and enjoyed playing word games with them.

Someone who investigated this area scientifically, back in the 1940s, was W.F. Leopold. Leopold carried out a thorough investigation of the pre-verbal linguistic development of a baby girl called Hildegard. The child was being brought up bilingually, but Leopold noticed, as he put it, that 'something had developed behind her words which was not simply identical with their phonetic complex or indissolubly tied to it ... the child at no time was a slave to words; she also focussed her attention on the sense behind phonetic configurations'.

Hildegard's first recorded utterances came at the age of 10 months and they were, according to Leopold, /piti/ and /da/. The utterance /piti/ he takes to mean 'pretty', and /da/ he takes to be a demonstrative pronoun, indicating 'there'.

From 13 months onwards, the morphosemantic element *DA*, in Hildegard's speech, begins to adhere to the category 'orientation towards others', an important adult morphosemantic category in English (and in Chinese). For Hildegard, it clearly comes to represent people she knows and takes an interest in (Jack, John, Jasper (*dadi*), Carolyn (*dada*), Gertrude (*deda*), and an aunt.) But it also occurs in *dash* 'cat' and *dai* 'dolly'. Reciprocity, another important adult orientational sub-category, also develops. It occurs in *dada* 'thank you'. Furthermore, *DA* comes to represent elongated objects: *dadi* is used for 'pencil' and 'stocking', and later for 'cover'. *DA* had been used for 'cover' as early as 13 months, and several months later was used for 'dress'. It could also be used to bracket 'cover' and 'stocking' together. Leopold wonders why Hildegard is so amused when her parents called her *Nackedei* ('naked child') on one occasion when she had no clothes on. Not embarrassment, surely. Not at one year and a few months. More likely *Nackedei*, which she recognises and reproduces as *dadi*, suggests to her not only that she is being addressed by a word that she uses for various males, but that she looks like some elongated object and is inexplicably clothed. Her parents must surely be pulling her leg. Hence the laughter.

Of course, by the age of 18 months a child is beginning to use full words. Though it is important to note that, as Jespersen, Leopold and others have noticed, the use of these words can be very far from the standard, and can embrace areas of meaning which in the adult language would be incongruous and illogical. Leopold particularly observed that the association between meanings and sounds were much less close in child language than in that of grown-ups.

Although our vocabulary is our most immediate and most interesting link with our environment, the actual mechanics of the process by which we learn it is something we are only beginning to find out about.

Notes and Suggested Further Reading

For Componential Analysis see G. Leech Semantics *(Harmondsworth, 1974), Chapter 6, or for a more sophisticated view, see J. Lyons* Semantics *(see Notes, etc. to Chapter 8 for reference), Chapter 9. See also J.J. Katz and J.A. Fodor:* Readings in the Philosophy of Language *(Englewood Cliffs, N.J., 1964). There are many excellent introductions to the acquisition of language by children. W.F. Leopold's study* Speech Development of a Bilingual Child: A Linguist's Record *(Evanston, Ill., 1949.) is not easy to come by as it has been long out of print. Two recent short introductions are M. Donaldson:* Children's Minds *(London, 1978) and A.J. Elliot:* Child Language *(Cambridge, 1981). My own paper on* 'The Learning of Vocabulary' *was published in* IRAL *(International Review of Applied Linguistics) Vol. 12 (3), 1974.*

10

CHOOSING BETWEEN WORDS

WORDS IN CONTEXT

When we are speaking we do not usually have the time, or the inclination, to consider why we use a particular word or turn of phrase. Only when we are writing do we have occasion to stop and think. If someone, looking over your shoulder, should ask why you expressed something that way, and not some other way, you might be inclined to reply if not: 'Go away and mind your own business', then: 'Well the word(s) *sound*(s) right, *feel*(s) right. That's what expresses most nearly what I wanted to say.'

In our last chapter we took a brief look at some of the internal factors which might lead us to a particular choice of word. It is now time to review some of the external factors governing our selection of words.

To what actual extent does *context* affect the meaning of a word?

Ludwig Wittgenstein, the Austrian philosopher who settled in Cambridge in the late 1920s, took an extreme view. In his opinion, the search for word meanings is futile and illusory, since the meaning of a word, he said, is none other than its *use* in the language. Wittgenstein compared a word to a piece in a game of chess. If we ask what is a king or a pawn or a rook in chess, we are not inquiring about the shape or size, the physical properties, of the pieces, but simply about their *function* in the game of chess. There is nothing inherently king-like about kings nor anything pawn-like about pawns in chess, since as pieces they represent only a set of possible moves prescribed by the rules of chess. 'There is a king' becomes meaningful only if we know what a piece in a game is.

According to Wittgenstein, language is a set of language games, and experiencing a word is just another such game. Our 'feeling' that a word has 'taken up its meaning into itself' — the semantic atmosphere of a word — is a private experience, and we communicate our own particular experience of what we mean by words without knowing if other people have any experience which is comparable.

An equally extreme approach, though poles apart from that of Wittgenstein, is that taken by J. R. Firth, a seminal British linguist, also active earlier this century. In Firth's view, a word is only incidentally an isolated lexical form. Mainly, and much more importantly, a word is a function of the 'context of situation' in which it occurs ('context of situation' is a term Firth borrowed from the more famous anthropologist Bronislaw Malinowski). Words, Firth agreed, do not occur in isolation, but in relation to what has already been said, to the circumstances in which they are spoken or written, to the individuals participating in a particular speech event, including what they are doing (or not doing) over and above speaking or writing. Words derive their meanings from those features of the real world indicated by the speech event and, lastly, from the effect achieved, or intended, by what is being said.

If what Firth said is correct, then every time a word is used in a new context of situation, it becomes a new word in disguise. If we want to have the meaning of the word *lion* we have hardly begun when we have looked up its meaning in the dictionary. We shall not have the *full* meaning of the word *lion* itself until we have exhausted the word's actual, and possible, contexts of situation.

The name of I.A. Richards has already been mentioned. Richards took a somewhat different view from Firth, arguing that words acquire meaning from the discourse in which they occur, rather than from context of situation. Discourse is different from context of situation in that it consists entirely of words and speech events. 'What a word means', says Richards, 'is the missing parts of the context from which it draws its delegated efficacy', the latter being a slightly cumbersome term to describe the abridgement of context that meaning actually is. To take a simple example: *The lion is a large quadruped of the feline species naturally existing in the wild, or tawny colour, with a tufted tail, the male having a shaggy mane.* Here the meaning of the word *lion* is *exactly* that given in the context. Here there are no missing parts. If we take a shorter sentence: *The keeper was mauled by a lion*, 'delegated efficacy' comes into operation, since there are obvious missing parts in the context: those parts contained in the earlier dictionary-like definition of a lion, together with other unstated predatory habits, and the fact that this particular lion is in captivity. Thus, according to Richards, all that words do is refer back to the missing parts of the context, any constancy of meaning being due only to the constancy of contexts. In the context of 'mauling' we expect lion, or similar animal. But *tiger* or *leopard* would have done just as well. *Sparrow* or *dolphin* would have been unacceptable in this particular context, since neither of these creatures 'mauls'. If we wanted to use either word we would have to provide support in the form of additional context.

In Richards' scheme the traditional relationship between word and sentence is entirely reversed. The meaning of a sentence becomes no longer the resultant effect of the meanings of its component words. The sentence determines meanings. It explains why the meaning of a word has to be guessed from the context each time it occurs. We only run to the dictionary when we are completely stumped.

Equally, a word is able, to a considerable extent, to 'predict' its environment, owing to a strong cohesive tendency between words. Firth had called this cohesive tendency *collocation*. The study of words and their lexical relations falls both within grammar and outside grammar. M.A.K. Halliday, influenced by Firth, has pointed out that lexical patterns do not even belong to grammar as such. For example, the words *strong, strength, strongly* and *strengthened* fall into quite different word classes: the first is an adjective, the second a noun, the third an adverb, the fourth a verb, or past participle. They not only function differently in the grammar for that very reason, but are not fully compatible semantically. (I can say *strong tea*, but not *She drank her tea strongly* nor *The tea had to be strengthened*.) Yet, from a *lexical* point of view, the four words are indisputably the same. What is abstracted from the four word-forms is an item *strong* having a scatter *strong, strongly, strength, strengthened*, which 'collocates' with items like *argue* and *tea*.

As far as the relationship between *strong* and *argue* is concerned, any grammatical relation may be quite irrelevant. They can, and often do, appear in different sentences, but may still be related through collocation as in: *I wasn't altogether convinced by his argument* followed closely by *He had some strong points to make but they couldn't all be substantiated*.

Halliday was one of the first to show that collocations between words do not occur in isolation. They 'collocate' as members of lexical 'sets'. Thus, for example, in the sentence *She is riding a horse*, *horse* belongs to a set which also includes *bicycle, motorbike, scooter*, and more peripherally, *hobby-horse, dolphin, camel, elephant* and many others. The peripheral members could be regarded as subsets, or might be better regarded as separate sets altogether. *She*, in the same sentence, would in the case of hobby-horse normally be restricted to a child, since riding dolphins, elephants or camels in not that common in Britain or the United States, and mostly requires rare expertise. Similarly, *riding* could be said to belong to a set which would also include *exercising, racing*, and possibly also *feeding* and *grooming*.

But what, you may well ask, is a lexical set? At first sight, the concept may strike us little more than an arbitrary device, because, in the main, lexical sets are open-ended, with no fixed membership. The chemical elements, the days of the week, kinship terms (within a particular culture) would form closed sets, but other sets would vary their membership according to the conditions (Firth's 'context of situation') in which they occur.

Nevertheless, three constants can probably be identified. Firstly, members of a lexical set would be expected to share a COMMON RANGE OF MEANING. In this way, *apple*, in a set with other fruits like *orange, pear*, etc. could be said to collocate with a set such as *sweet, sour*, or with some other set, which would include *round, spherical*, etc; with still another containing *green, red, greenish*, etc. Secondly, members of the same lexical set could be expected to share a COMMON FACTOR OF DENOTATION; in other words, to denote, more or less, the same kind of object. One such set would be: [*taxi, car, automobile, lorry, jeep*, etc.] all of which share the common factor: 'a four-wheeled vehicle driven by internal combustion'. If *train, tram* or *cart* were to be admitted to this set, the common factor would have to be broadened to something like 'wheeled vehicle moved by some form of power (whether internal combustion, electricity, mechanical, or animal)'. Attempts to extend set membership beyond a certain limit would so extend the common factor of denotation that it would cease to have any value. Thirdly, a lexical set will consist of words belonging to the same WORD CLASS (nouns, or transitive verbs, or adjectives, etc.) or having a SIMILAR GRAMMATICAL FUNCTION. Thus, *here, there* and *everywhere* could be said to belong to the same lexical set in this sense. To sum up, then, a lexical set is not arbitrary, as it is subject to at least three constraints: COMMON RANGE OF MEANING, COMMON DENOTATION, AND GRAMMATICAL FUNCTION.

What makes lexical sets particularly interesting is that they interact with context to produce 'text'. The factors that govern this interface lie outside language. Thus in any collocation there is always an 'extralinguistic' as well as a linguistic dimension. The lexical sets are regulated by linguistic factors, but the actual interface with context, including other lexical sets, is not.

These 'extralinguistic' factors may be grouped, for convenience, into *social, cultural* and *geographical*. In English, for example, it is not difficult to propose a collocational relationship between members of the sets [*orange, apple, pear*, etc.] and [*sweet, succulent*, etc.]. But in standard British English, *lemon* would be excluded from the 'fruit' set, because in Britain lemons do not ripen sufficiently to taste sweet. In the Caribbean, however, where lemons ripen, the situation is different. Here, we are up against a *geographical* constraint.

On the other hand, all fruits, including lemons, collocate with members of the closed set [*ripe, unripe*]. But, in most languages, the fruit set would also include 'people'. In English, however, 'unripe' people are referred to as *immature*. English thus needs an extra set [*mature, immature*] to collocate with people. Here, we have a cultural constraint, arising from the *cultural* peculiarities of the English language, which divides up the universe slightly differently from that of neighbouring languages like French or German or Welsh.

Finally, in Britain for example, the set [*ripe, unripe*] collocates with *cheese*; but only under certain conditions. Most native English cheeses do not ripen. If left lying around long enough they only get dry or mouldy. The frequency of collocation of *cheese* with [*ripe, unripe*] will therefore vary, depending on the social habits, tastes, and possibly even the social class of the user. Only speakers eating more expensive imported cheeses would use this particular 'ripeness' collocation with any frequency. Here we are faced with a *social* constraint primarily.

Are there any limits to collocation? It is thought that there are limits, but that these limits are neither linguistic nor contextual, having more to do with what McIntosh has called 'tolerated ranges of collocability'. The edges of this range of tolerance are, admittedly, vague, and are bound to be unstable; the whole question of compatibility being very complicated. If we compare the sentences: (1) *The molten postage feather scored a weather*, and (2) *The flaming waste-paper basket snored violently*, we will immediately agree that (2) is more acceptable than (1), though neither of course is readily acceptable. McIntosh thinks sentence (1) has to be rejected because it has 'departed from tolerated ranges of collocability'. In the spirit of Firth, he further argues that the inventory of nouns, for example, that can be qualified by the adjective *molten* is just as much as part of the language as is the grammatical system, so much more fully studied by linguistics; and that a full account of this set or inventory goes a long way towards constituting the meaning of 'molten'. According to such a view, no word is an isolate, but a summation of the collocational relationships it can establish with other words in the language.

But this takes us into the complexities of the notion of acceptability and semantic normativeness. Poets especially, sometimes take us well beyond the limits of tolerance, and more

81

'difficult' poets in this sense may require of us a very long period of time before we come to terms with them and their work, which will eventually push back the established limits.

Notes and Suggested Further Reading

J.R. Firth's views are well represented in Papers in Linguistics 1934-1951 *(London, 1957), particularly Nos. 3, 10, 14, 15 and 16. See also P. Strevens, A. McIntosh and M.A.K. Halliday:* Patterns of Language: Papers in General, Descriptive and Applied Linguistics *(London, 1966), especially 'Paper One' and 'Paper Eleven'; also Halliday's paper 'Lexis as a linguistic level' in C.E. Bazell (ed.):* In Memory of J.R. Firth *(London, 1966). Wittgenstein's main arguments appear in his* Philosophical Investigations *(Oxford, 1953). The reference for I.A. Richards:* The Philosophy of Rhetoric *is (2nd Edn., New York, 1950).*

McIntosh's article 'Patterns and Ranges' could be read in conjunction with William Empson's The Structure of Complex Words *(London, 1964).*

11

ON THE TIP OF ONE'S TONGUE

It could prove to be that the language and lexicon at our command reflect in large part the structure and function of our brain and nervous system.

The terms 'structure' and 'function' are being used with a special purpose. In language, as in much other human activity, structure and function are separate from each other. As we have seen, our lexicons in particular are very delicately structured, enabling us to make rather subtle choices between alternatives. *I can be firm* sounds good, *I am obstinate* less so; and *I am pigheaded* is something one would never say about oneself, except in joking. Yet, *firm*, *obstinate*, and *pigheaded* have a common denotation. If I am struggling to communicate in a foreign language I don't know too well, I can get by with surprisingly few words and phrases, and a minimal command of the grammar. Even in normal instances, we can notice that words or phrases that have a specific structure can express different functions. In the sentences: *Where are you going? I am going to the supermarket*, the structure and function of the verbs *are going/am going* are the same. The structure prescribes 'present tense continuous: in the process of'. Function likewise. But in the sentence *Tomorrow I am going to a concert*, the function

83

of 'am going' is 'future time: planning to go'. In English, *were* from a structural point of view indicates simple past tense. In a sentence like *If I were you, I would do this* 'were' suggests a different function: some kind of conditional future time. And in *Men were deceivers ever* the 'were' is equivalent in function to 'have (always) been', a kind of perpetual present.

This absence of congruity between structure and function results in great adaptability. If for example a language loses almost all its (structural) declensional system — as English did in the Middle Ages — the functions of that system can be taken over by prepositions, articles, adverbs and so forth. If a language loses a word, the displacement is not serious because the functional side of things can cope with the loss. English is about to lose the *meaning* of *disinterested*, because most people nowadays use it interchangeably with *uninterested*. But there are plenty of alternative means of expressing 'disinterestedness' in the language. Sometimes *unbiased* will serve; in other cases *neutral*. Cumbersome phrases like *conflict of interest* may have to be invoked. The point is that there is no need to fuss; we can manage. Learners of Chinese are sometimes perplexed by the fact that the Chinese language has no plurals. How can the Chinese 'manage' without plurals? Well, they can and do manage very well. So much so that, before long, the learner cannot remember that there ever was a problem.

In all living things, structure and function are in dynamic balance. Too much emphasis on structure would lead to a dangerous rigidity, 'doing things always by the book'; and on the other hand, over-preoccupation with function could lead to anarchy. There is too the important interface between the two. Without this interface we could not have sentences like *Men were deceivers ever*, but only *Men have always been deceivers*, which is very nearly, but somehow not quite, the same. The point we are leading round to is that structure and function are different aspects of a single *system*. Living systems, we might need to remind ourselves, also continuously interact in crucial ways with the environment.

What has so far been said about language applies in comparable ways to the brain and the central nervous system.

The most famous proponent of localised centres of the brain

was the great nineteenth-century physician Broca. The brain was mapped into a series of areas, each responsible for a particular activity: hearing, speech, writing, taste, and so forth. Broca's 'structural' picture of the brain remains to a large extent valid, and it can be shown that electrical stimulus of successive areas of the brain result in largely predictable responses in the subject. The most important concept to have survived intact is that of the left and right cerebral hemispheres, each of which is associated with dominance of different brain functions.

A less popularly known contemporary of Broca was Hughlings Jackson. Jackson took a very different view from that of Broca: a functional view. Jackson believed that the brain and central nervous system operate as a whole, and that no defect can be fully explained in terms of localisation, but only as something that affects the organism as a whole in its relation to the environment, the entire physiology and personality of the individual. More recently, the central nervous system has been described as a dynamically ordered economy of behavioural response and adjustment. The modern view is that the brain is not only genetically preprogrammed but, more important, a continuously self-reprogramming system — a biological, as opposed to electronic, computer. The brain consists of an extraordinary network of points at which functional connections are made (synapses), and unimaginably complex and sensitive feedback circuits, governed by a reticular system which serves as a filter.

As was pointed out earlier, the old linguistic model of the brain picking up a message, decoding it, and encoding a reply now seems far too simple. We are dealing not with a machine but something far different, and immensely more complex. What happens, in crude terms, is that, on detecting an incoming auditory signal, the central nervous system goes rapidly and circularly through a series of matchings until a suitable response can be made. This matching is effected by means of an 'internalized model' which undergoes constant modification or 'recoding' until the incoming input and the model merge. The response may be a return utterance, or a perception, or a thought, or emotional responses of various kinds.

It can be seen that message reception is not passive, but active and creative. Incoming speech signals are not just 'heard' and then 'decoded'. They are recreated in our own kinaesthetic nervous pathways and speech organs, before they can be understood. This is from start to finish a process of simulation, and what neurologists term 'motor recreation'.

Nowadays, we can appreciate that language function in the individual is extremely delicately adjusted. An infinitesimal disruption of feedback functions, or of the timing of tightly synchronised events, or a slight delay in 'gating' functions can lead to overloading of circuits, which can in turn result in disturbances of speech or hearing. These may be temporary or long-lasting, depending on the nature and gravity of the underlying causes. Too much alcohol will produce a temporary disturbance of speech; but a massive brain haemorrhage can produce disturbance not only of language but of other brain functions such as memory and muscular coordination from which the patient, especially if advanced in years, may have difficulty in achieving complete recovery, even with the best of therapy.

In fact, language disturbance ranges all the way from an ordinary nagging search for a missing word on the tip of one's tongue — which is something nearly all of us experience — to a complex and near-complete loss of language function. It is difficult to draw a hard-and-fast boundary between 'normal' and 'pathological' disturbances, particularly as a great deal depends on the individual and the circumstances. Inability to cope is probably the main indicator in most cases; and again, many normal people may fall below the pathological limit, if only temporarily, as a result of shock, fatigue or stress. Serious cases are associated with brain haemorrhages, brain tumours, or other form of organic damage, but also with quite severe trauma, like shell shock, for instance.

The most complex disorders of language are covered by the term *aphasia*. Aphasia is the term used for a wide range of acquired language disorders occurring in people whose speech and language has previously been normal.

Aphasia can be roughly described as something resulting from localised brain damage, but which often has associated with it widespread impairment of language function, reducing the likelihood that a person communicating with another person or persons will be able to understand or produce appropriate verbal responses. Aphasia is an area of medical science that has been completely transformed by the application of linguistic models to its investigation, analysis, and diagnosis. But, conversely, linguistics itself has started to gain from the insights achieved by speech therapists and neurologists in the investigation of this complex phenomenon.

The many different classifications of aphasia proposed by clinicians have borne out the reality of the linguist's claims for the syntactic, phonological, semantic, lexical and pragmatic categories of language. Even the axes of simultaneity (paradigmatic) and sequence (syntagmatic), so strongly argued by Roman Jakobson, have retained their validity in aphasia classification. The lexicon especially can be most profoundly affected by disorders of simultaneity. A word like *language* in the speech of a patient can occur as *lunging*, *lungage*, or even *longing* or *luggage*(? unintended irony). Semantic categories, even quite basic ones like wife, daughter or mother, can become uncertain. There is, for instance, a long-established test, called the 'Colour Sorting Test', administered to patients who have previously been tested for colourblindness, and found to be still normal in that particular respect. In this test, patients are asked to sort a pile of different coloured strips of material. Even though not colour-blind, patients with severe language disturbance will not be able to sort with any degree of reliability. This means that the patient is unable to distinguish reliably for instance between green and blue, or between red and yellow, because his language — not his eyes — will not allow him to do so.

From the point of view of the aphasiologist, however, it would appear that an aphasia-based categorisation of language would probably be in two parts. These two parts would correspond to two types of language disorder. The first of these (Type A) is relatively superficial and takes the form of a reduced rate of verbal articulation, with word associations remaining normal, even if these words tend to be all high frequency commonly used items, as if lexical sets (see earlier discussion in the previous chapter) had been compressed or severely reduced. Type B represents a more profound disturbance of language in which, oddly enough, the rate of emission of speech increases, yet word associations become bizarre.

'Type A' disorders might be said to correspond to the linguistic areas of lexical morphology, phonology, and syntactic morphology. These areas are, for the linguist, intricate enough. Lexical morphology would have do with the matters we discussed in Chapter 8, phonology with Chomsky's identifiable 'phonological component', and syntactic morphology with syntactic transformations. 'Type B' disorders, on the other hand, have to do with the 'deep structures' of language, with propositions, meanings; but also with extra-linguistic functions like memory, feeling, attitudes and perceptions.

No doubt, in time, we shall have far more adequate models of language structure and function than we have at present, and these models will have incorporated or, at any rate, been influenced by the empirical evidence gathered from research into aphasic disorders of language. At the same time, and even more important, the linguist will be guided into other areas of human activity (and into making creative links with related disciplines) of which language forms an integral part. Linguists have sometimes needed reminding that, although aphasia may in one sense be a linguistic problem, the aphasic patient is a medical problem of much wider extent, since aphasia rarely occurs in isolation from other physiological and neurological disturbances.

And this brings us back to where we started yet another brief excursion. Just as language must be viewed not as a self-enclosed phenomenon with its own structures, rules and mechanisms, but as an only partly separable entity, integrally interwoven with the whole of the human being and environment; so too must the brain be seen within the context of the same human situation. Men of science, be they linguists or neurophysiologists, may be tempted from time to time with panaceas opened up by routine mechanical methods, artificially controlled environments, or dogmatic procedures. (Capable children, for example, spend years in sterile school classroom environments, or equally sterile 'language laboratories', learning foreign languages which they fail to master). Today's speech therapist knows that recovery from language loss can only occur in an environment that provides motivation, stimulation and exercise. In fact the human organism can be expected to right itself and to bring itself to normal performance, provided only that it is aided to the utmost to do so. Aphasic children can more readily achieve this than elderly adults, partly because their brain functions are more supple and adaptable, but partly also because attitudes do not impede, and because of the quality of the perceived environment, which for the child is richer than it is for the ageing adult.

Notes and Suggested Further Reading

The most readable book on language pathology is by Ruth Lesser: Linguistic Investigations of Aphasia *(London, 1978). An excellent but moderately difficult account of the function of his brain and the central nervous system is given in the first section of M.F. Berry:* Language Disorders of Children *(Englewood Cliffs, N.J., 1969). Other provocative accounts and explanations of language disturbance, including some of the approaches developed by Jakobson, are in A.V.S. de Reuck and M. O'Connor (eds.):* Disorders of Language *(London, 1964).*

12

THE WRITTEN WORD

Writing is something we take so much for granted that we are unlikely to be aware of the extent to which it has pervaded language as a whole.

There was a time, not so many years ago, when some linguists naively supposed that speech and writing existed alongside each other, on parallel tracks. Speech could be converted into writing by simply transcribing what is being said; and writing converted into speech by simply reading aloud from a text.

This may still be to some extent true of *modern* speech which, as already pointed out, is so heavily influenced by writing. But, even today, a gap exists. If you have ever had the task of transcribing — i.e. committing to writing —from a tape-recorder perhaps, a natural piece of speech, especially dialogue, you will have experienced the frustration well-known to all transcribers. Instead of speech, consisting of neat sentences, with phrases succeeding one another in orderly fashion, you are confronted with silences, meaningless huh's and ha's, and disjointed, not even properly finished, phrases and sentences. With dialogue, the situation can be even worse: quite often the speakers do not give each other time to finish, before taking their next turn.

The reverse process can be just as puzzling, but different. Readers who can read perfectly well are sometimes notoriously unable to capture the naturalness of speech. Even poets are sometimes surprisingly bad at reciting their own work. A large part of the reason for this is that writing takes little or no account of varieties of pause length, stress patterns, intonation, vocal nuance, and other features of natural speech. Broadcasters, even those with a reasonable flair for the job, usually need to be specially trained.

In today's world it would be quite hard to find speakers who have not been influenced by writing. Even the illiterate watch television, and listen to the radio. And as for peoples who have not yet succumbed to the modern electronic media, even they possess a usually highly developed oral literature. For remnants of the original discrepancy between spoken and written language we may look to certain American film sound-tracks which have emphasised natural speech, or we might even take a fresh look at what Bernstein, the British sociologist, detected among present-day urban communities: an 'elaborated' code, often associated with middle-class people, and a 'restricted' code, more typical of the working class. The latter is predominantly spoken language, poor in vocabulary, but surprisingly complex and mercurial in syntax and heavily punctuated by gestural, deictic expressions. To take one example, Bernstein has given this as an example of 'restricted' code:

> 'It's all according like these youths and that if they get into these gangs and that they must have a bit of lark around and say it goes wrong and that they probably knock someone off I mean think they just do it to be big getting publicity here and there.

This can be rendered into a certain kind of standard English, an 'elaborated' code, as:

> 'Some of today's young people join gangs, indulge in mischief, and may kill someone inadvertently, merely to attract attention to themselves.'

The difficulty in locating, actually 'hearing', true speech is so great that some writers have developed consummate skill in creating the 'illusion' of real talk. Modern writers as different as Faulkner, Joyce, Pinter and Salinger have succeeded in this, though the tradition is an old one, traceable in English at least as far as back in time as Chaucer. The Russian novelist Gogol created such a perfect illusion, that many Russians are convinced that Gogol's dialogue is totally really speech. It is only on closer inspection of the text that they find his language literary, sometimes to a grotesque degree.

The point I have been making is that the language of writing is the one to which we have continual access. The language of speaking on the other hand is quite remote from our everyday experience. Westerners who chance upon oral cultures can be surprised by the degree of value and care that oral communities invest in their cultivation of the spoken word. It is on record for instance that pueblo Indians of the south-west of the United States distrust attempts to put their speech into writing for fear of the mistakes and sacrifices implicit in the written word. They are above all afraid that writing may introduce a new force into their lives.

There probably never has been a time, or place, ever since the emergence of modern man (*Homo Sapiens*), with his fully-fledged language, when oral literature was completely absent. Indeed, it may be a basic condition that, before grammar and vocabulary as related systems can develop, some form of memorised oral literary tradition allowing for a degree of improvisation, for song and rhythm must be present. As we saw earlier, anthropologists like Leroi-Gourhan have argued, plausibly, that the palaeolithic cave paintings and rock inscriptions represent early forms of 'writing'. The complex designs of animals and occasional human figures would form the 'texts' that would be 'read' by the initiated at certain seasons and on prescribed occasions. The late Bruce Chatwin has given a recent and vivid account of how Australian Aboriginals, only in very recent times shaken out of their Old Stone Age mode of life, learn sets of 'songs', each of which associated with a particular location along a 'songline'; the set of songs actually learned depending on the ancestral totem of the particular individual. Two individuals belonging to different totems, say a Wallaby or Emu ancestral totem, will have different songlines. When members of the same totem meet on their wanderings they may exchange 'songs' according to very precise prosodic rules, which may not be infringed, even on pain of death.

How and why, then, did these oral traditions, first in one area, later in others, and in modern times almost everywhere, give way to the written word and the Book?

The transition must have been quite gradual, for we know that within the same society oral traditions survived by many many centuries the arrival of writing. One explanation for this relatively peaceful co-existence is that the use of writing was confined to calendars, records, inventories, ritual and comparable purposes. The bardic domain remained oral until relatively modern times, when finally the written word gained precedence there also.

'Conditions arose in history ... where experience has to be recorded: we need to store knowledge, and put it on file. So we invent a filing system for language, reducing it to writing. The effect of this is to anchor language at a shallower level of consciousness. For the first time, language comes to be made of constituents — sentences — instead of dependency patterns — clause complexes — of the spoken mode. And with constituency comes a different form of the interpretation of experience.

'Writing' must have moved into a qualitatively very different dimension with the invention of script as such — 'logographic' or ideographic writing. Writing was invented, independently, in various parts of the globe in late Neolithic times: in China, in the Indus Valley, in Egypt and Sumer, and much later in Central America, by the Mayas. The earliest forms of logographic writing were definitely associated with records, especially calendrical records, and no doubt had a close association with the development of agriculture, village communities, and larger political units, which allowed for specialisation: priesthoods, ruling castes, and the various trades and occupations of the village, and the larger township or city.

Logographic writing constitutes one of the major world

revolutions, at least as significant as the Scientific and Industrial Revolutions which followed several millennia later. The logograph — what the Chinese call the 'character' and the Egyptologist termed the hieroglyph — forced speech into certain rather fixed moulds. Once you had logographs for sun and moon, for day and night, for field, tree and stream, you placed certain logical restrictions on the speaker and his language. He could not, for instance, be here now, both a magus sitting in rapt contemplation, and a hawk flying in the distant sky. His inner life or 'spirit' could not go on being the same thing as the 'wind' blowing out there. He was forced to concede that 'the blowing of the inner spirit' was ... well ... a metaphor.

Of course, logographic writing still left the speaker a good deal of latitude. Take pronunciation, for example, and in particular, the case of Modern Chinese. The character ('person') in Northern China is pronounced 'ren', whereas in Canton and Hong Kong it is pronounced 'yan'. Moreover, the syntax could be highly fluid, with a relative absence of prepositions, articles, conjunctions, and the like; with the result that much scope was left to the reader as interpreter. We know what certain passages in Chinese poems were reliably intended to mean only by referring to commentators who handed down a tradition of interpretation. In their perversity, modern readers would often choose to ignore these commentaries and evolve something far more exciting: their *own* interpretation.

The complete synchronisation between speech and writing — alphabetic writing — was only a matter of time. The process began somewhere in the Eastern Mediterranean in the late second millennium B.C. It is especially associated with the Phoenicians, who are themselves unlikely however to have evolved alphabetic writing. But, because of their extensive maritime trading links in the Mediterranean and beyond, it is most likely that the Phoenicians are the ones to have disseminated this form of writing, especially the specific alphabetised forms that developed first into the Greek alphabet, and later into the Etruscan and Roman scripts.

From this time forward, the discourse of writing completely permeated the spoken medium. And after the invention of moveable-type printing in the 15th century the language of letters became the property of all who had a modicum of education. In the Western world the concept of schooling itself was a by-product of the invention of alphabetic writing. Poets, particularly those more turbulent and adventurous ones who have tried to burst the bonds of the alphabetic writing straitjacket, have felt the constraints more deeply than any.

Modern alphabetic writing has invaded languages that are not even alphabetic, like Chinese, or only partially alphabetic, like Japanese. The process cannot be stopped. Chinese, to take one instance, has already a well-established passive voice, and it is likely to go on acquiring the best logico-syntactic forms, wherever these make writing better ordered and better suited to modern urban technological conditions. Only the very high concentration of homophones — possibly a legacy from a time before writing — has prevented Chinese from adopting the Roman alphabet, despite the fact that it has been possible to 'romanise' all Chinese words, it now being common practice for Chinese dictionaries to include romanised vocabulary items, and in some cases even to arrange the listings in alphabetical order.

When the claim is sometimes made that pre-literate and literate peoples are 'brain different', it is not always a racist claim. The fact that urbanised Westerners speak more or less as they write is bound to affect the way in which the individual's brain has formed. He (or she) is likely to be more intelligent (in the IQ sense) than sharp-witted, more organised than resourceful, sensible rather than spontaneous. The seeming riot and chaos of real speech is something unfamiliar to most literate people, whose grammar is for them the only grammar. The grammar of the grammarians must always be the grammar of the written language, or some notional norm which has all the features of a written (usually from earlier literary dialects) language. As soon as I stop to think what I am saying, I am reaching for a written norm. Notions of correctness, explicitness, rhetorical well-formedness are absent from spoken language, whose norms are those of the village, the street locality, the speech fellowship of the pub or the pool room, shifting from day to day, from place to place, from one group of people to another.

At this point, perhaps, we should distinguish between educated literate speech, truly spoken language, and what is often called a vernacular. Although a vernacular, initially at least, is a purely spoken language, it has in fact arisen in a vacuum lying somewhere between literate speech and real (non-literate) speech. A vernacular is a regularisation, a formalisation of non-literate speech. It comes into being when literate speech has been perceived to be too remote from spoken language, but where there is a need for literate, even if as yet unwritten, norms. Left to develop in its own right, and without over-dominance from the official literate norm, a vernacular will eventually produce its own poets and writers. This happened with all the so-called 'Romance' languages — French, Italian, Spanish, Portuguese, etc. — which departed in the early Middle Ages from their 'Roman' or Latin norm. It is happening today to some extent with modern languages, like spoken French for example, which has been found to have developed quite different ways of saying things from those of textbook French. In some cultures, vernaculars have only appeared in limited social domains. For instance, for a very long time there has been a well-developed vernacular of Chinese known as Cantonese. It is so different from standard Chinese that many linguists consider it a separate language altogether. Cantonese, officially at least, has no written form, even though most Cantonese words that do not occur in standard Chinese do have their own written characters. In other words, you will not find novels written, or newspapers printed, in Cantonese.

In case you are thinking a vernacular literary norm cannot evolve out of slovenly, ill-educated speech, like that, say, of the pre-reformed Eliza Doolittle, a glance at some of the bits of Latin that ended up in the vernacular Latin written norm that we recognize as Modern French might set you thinking.

Classical Latin like most classical languages was purist in its approach to grammar. A tense was a tense, and a paradigm a paradigm, and paradigms were pure and unmixed. Yet, in *spoken* Latin the use of *habere* 'to have' with the infinitive to form future imperfect and perfect tenses was so widespread that every Romance language has developed its tense system from these bastardised compounds. Spoken Latin even used *essere habeo* 'I have to be' as a future tense (French *je serai*, Ital. *saro*, etc.) Classical Latin did make use of *ille*, the demonstrative adjective meaning 'that', but only for emphasis. In spoken Latin however the use of *ille* must have been so widespread that it developed into the definitive article 'the' (French *le*, Ital. *lo*, Romanian *-l*) and also into the third person subject and object pronoun 'he, she, it' (French *il, le*, Ital. *lo*, etc.) If you really wanted to emphasise something in spoken Latin, you had to say *ecce ille* 'behold, that' (French *cela*). This reminds us of creations like *splendiferous, superstar, king-size*, when the usual epithets (*splendid, star, large*) have been commercially devalued. Classical Latin had a whole range of single word adverbs (e.g. *simul* 'at the same time', *ubi* 'where', *interim* 'in the meantime', etc.). Spoken Latin, by contrast, felt the need to strengthen these with the addition of a preposition: *ubi* becomes *de ubi* 'from where' (Ital. *dove*); *simul* shows up as *in simul* (French *ensemble*, Ital. *insieme*); *interim* adds *dum* (Ital. *(do)mentre*, Span. *(do)mentrias*) which in English would be something like 'while in the meantime'. The perfectly good *saepe* 'often' was replaced by *subinde* 'then thereupon' (French *souvent*).

Since the arrival of civilisation, language has generally tended towards written language. It may even transpire that writing is a precondition for the consolidated growth of civilisation. 'Writing brings language to consciousness', says Halliday. 'Writing puts language in chains; it freezes it, so that it becomes a *thing* to be reflected on. Writing deprives language of the power to intuit, to make indefinitely many connections in different directions at once, to explore contradictions, to represent experience as fluid and indeterminate. It is therefore destructive of one fundamental human potential: to think on your toes, as we put it'. At the same time, writing has given human beings immense power. Also it has given them the possibility of building their spiritual and communal lives. Without The Book we would have none of the world's great religions, no laws, no learning. Without books we would not even have our private lives. As the one of Dostoevsky's characters said:

> 'Leave us alone without any books, and we at once get confused, lose ourselves in a maze, not knowing what to cling to, what to hold on to, what to love and what to hate, what to respect and what to despise.'

Notes and Suggested Further Reading

It would be hard to name a single work covering this area. I earlier mentioned Léroi-Gourhan's classic study Le Geste et la Parole *(see above). Derrida's work must be relevant, but is not easy to read (in French or in English). His* Grammatology *(Baltimore, 1974) has been translated. A plain man's short guide to the history of writing is given in Bolinger and Sear's* Aspects of Language, *Chapter 11 (see above). The full reference for Bernstein's* Class, Codes and Control *is (London 1971, or 1973). See also Bruce Chatwin* Song Lines *(London, 1987).*

Quite a number of interesting essays, including the one by Halliday, are included in N. Fabb, et al: The Linguistics of Writing *(Manchester, 1987).*

13

WORDS AND THE POET

One of the more important outcomes of modern linguistic analysis, whether in linguistics proper or in the philosophy of language, is that we now possess a fair understanding of what words are, or at any rate what words are *not*. Those engaged in the study of literature, on the other hand, have been aware all along, implicitly at least, that the word cannot be handled by methods appropriate to the dissecting table.

The elusive, supradimensional nature of the word is something most poets, writers and critics take for granted. When the early twentieth-century French poet Paul Valéry said that literature is made of language, he was not even hinting that students of literature ought to go off and study linguistics or linguistic philosophy. Nor is the student of literature straying into disciplines he knows little about when he makes frequent reference to the *language* of a text or an author. Coleridge was surely not thinking of dictionaries when he wrote that literature is 'the best words in the best order'. Nor is Northrop Frye about to enter the lists with linguists or lexicographers when he compares the 'order of words' with the order of nature investigated by natural scientists. No branch of learning has a monopoly on the word, and the inner sanctum is still the preserve of the poet, the 'creator' *par excellence*.

Before going on, however, one comment is called for. In modern times, the poet is not simply a writer of metrical verse. He may not write in verse at all, but may be a novelist, or a dramatist, or a writer of short stories. Sometimes, as with Richard Jefferies or Thoreau or W.H. Hudson, he may not even be a writer of prose fiction. And in more recent times we should not overlook the journalist, or even the advertisement copywriter. Poetry is not the privilege any more of cultured circles, but the property of Everyman. For that reason we now experience the breadth of the creative spirit in every kind of discourse, whether it be in the high realm of Eliot's *Four Quartets* or in the more accessible Beatles, and their successors. From now on therefore we will be using the term poet in this wider sense.

At some very distant time in the past, everyone was a poet, and no one was a poet. Poets were everywhere, but they were anonymous. The trees, rocks, springs and animals spoke, and everyone could answer them, producing a uniquely individual world where anyone 'could be' potentially at least, anything. Gradually — we have no idea how or over what vista of time — sacred lore crystallised out of this 'blooming buzzing' complexity and, though it remained the secret property of the totemic clan, here was the beginning of literature. As with the Australian Aboriginal of today, an individual, at his initiation, would have inherited a set of 'songs', which he in turn passed on to succeeding generations. In late Neolithic and Bronze Age times, with the coming into being of larger societies, this literature lost most or all of its arcane value and evolved into epic: epics such as the Iliad, Gilgamesh, or the Bhagavad Gita. Finally, with the invention of writing, the poet comes into his (or her) own as the creator of the sacrosanctly individual poetic product. We moderns go on finding it difficult to conceive that Homer may have been several different 'poets'.

Today's poet continues to achieve what entire groups of pre-literate peoples achieved in their communal language. Indeed, the languages we inherited from our forebears are compacted of the very ingredients that, in a literate age, have become poetic devices.

One of these ingredients is *metaphor*; another is its complement which, by rolling several rhetorical categories into one, Roman Jakobson has been intent on calling *metonymy*.

Metaphor first, then. Whenever I apply a word associated with a particular object — say, a *leaf* on a plant or tree — to a *different* object — a 'leaf' or page in a book, I am making use of metaphor. In this instance, the botanical meaning is said to be the 'literal' meaning, and the page leaf the 'figurative' meaning. To achieve truly original success with this standard kind of metaphor, I would not only have to have a sense of appropriacy but a very rare kind of rhetorical skill.

This is the classical view, dating back at least to the time of Aristotle, but one that in recent times has been challenged. According to more recent thinking, a metaphor is not the taking on of a special new meaning, not something too novel for literal expression but, in Ricoeur's words, 'the metaphor's deviations from normal discourse belong to the great enterprise of "saying what is".' If this were not the case, the metaphor would simply have degenerated into a dispensable ornament, losing itself in language games.

According to Ricoeur, the 'page' meaning is just as essentially a part of the meaning of *leaf* as the botanical meaning. Nowadays we think of metaphor as an integral part of language; the origin of logical thought and the root of all classification. Through metaphor, Ricoeur insists, poetry does have the power of making contact with reality. The potential meaning, or range of connotation, of words is without limit. Discussing the English divine, Jeremy Taylor's metaphor, 'virginity is the life of angels, the enamel of the soul', Ricoeur explains that something previous to the creation of this metaphor had been happening in the language. Various properties of 'enamel' that had never been clearly recognised before as connotations of that word had been accruing to the language all the while.

All language, in fact, 'makes' and 'remakes' the world. The alleged distinction between metaphoric and literal statement can easily be shown to be illusory. Not only do the propositions of science have cognitive validity; but aesthetic experience, feelings and emotions also. Otherwise, we would never be able to communicate to each other the most elementary sensations, like toothaches or other physical sensations, or everyday likes and dislikes.

A corollary to what has just been claimed is that meaning in literature has the same validity as the language of descriptive statement. Invariance of meaning in ordinary discourse, which is mistakenly supposed to be flat and one-dimensional, is itself a fiction, since the whole of our language is undergoing constant change in a continually expanding world and consciousness. The supposedly 'universal' symbols that are being signalled to other possible solar systems in the galaxy, if they ever do encounter another superhuman intelligence, will at best betray the current state of our own consciousness and language (in the widest sense).

The whole dichotomy between literal and figurative, which as we have implied goes back to Classical Greece, arose from a logical misconception. Because we are able to notice metaphors in the process of being created, we have wrongly assumed that in pre-literate, pre-logical times all words must have had literal meanings and that their 'poets' created metaphors just as we do. Whereas in reality, once we delve back in time, we come up against a world of *different* presuppositions: a world of concrete meanings we cannot accommodate, which have had to be split up in order to survive in modern consciousness.

At one time, for example, we know that the Greek word *pneuma* must have meant 'breath', 'spirit' and 'wind'. To *us* it means three discrete things. To a pre-literate distant ancestor of the Athenian Greeks *pneuma* expressed a meaning in which breath, spirit and wind were not yet separate or separable. As Owen Barfield has put it:

> 'We must imagine a time in which 'spiritus' or *pneuma* or older words from which these words were descended meant neither *breath*, nor *wind*, nor *spirit*, nor yet all three of these things, but when they simply had *their own old peculiar meaning*, which has since, in the course of the evolution of consciousness, crystallised into the three meanings specified'

What the modern poet, according to Barfield, is doing is letting us glimpse these realities again. Poetry has changed, along with the human beings that produce it. The older poetic principle gave way before the rational principle, according to which meaning had to be split up. (You could not have a single word meaning 'wind', 'spirit' and 'breath' any more). This change, over a long period of time, was accompanied by an equally long awakening from unconsciousness to full consciousness.

The poetic process, according to Barfield, is more than a rediscovery of ancient meanings: it is a regeneration of meaning, the creation of new meanings, through the constant creative activity of metaphor. The poet is not simply a restorer. He has to embrace different realms of our experience, and blend them into a seamless unity.

Metaphor, thus, is not be thought of as a mere rhetorical device, nor even as a device confined to poetry. On the contrary, every fresh use of a word is metaphorical: a shift in sense, albeit a small one. All this is made possible because, although many words have fragmented into a range of different senses, these innumerable senses never exhaust the potentialities inherent in a particular word. Each word, it has been said, carries within it a 'metaphorical spring', and each time it is used the qualification 'something like' is implied. Even a simple statement like: 'This is water' conceals a whole repertoire of knowledge, both scientific and poetic. Furthermore, if somebody contradicts me and says: 'What you call water is really virtual empty space', I will either dismiss what I am being told as fantasy, or will know that some scientific-poetic metaphor belonging to modern physics is being invoked.

Meanings are not ghostly entities accompanying actual words. They are, as it were, (forgive the metaphor!) the 'landscape' of a word. They are rooted in the setting of a word, in all its collocations, connotations and associations; they are also rooted in our own past. When Shakespeare (Barfield reminds us) uses the word *ruin* in 'The noble ruin of her magic, Antony' he is reviving a very ancient sense of 'ruin' which is still barely audible in its Latin etymon 'swift disastrous movement', but at the same time Shakespeare transformed 'ruin' into a 'warm and living thing, a rich piece of imaginative material ready at hand for anyone who has the skill to evoke its power.' With Shakespeare, *ruin* recaptured

103

an aura which had virtually disappeared, but now was given a fresh, and enhanced, lease of life.

The poetic partner, and complement of metaphor, is *metonymy* (in the extended sense used by Jakobson). Metonymy has to do with the *contiguity* of words, the easily observable fact that words usually and naturally occur in the vicinity of others. Words regularly in contiguity have a tendency to develop a particular affinity with each other, particularly if they occur in regular phrases. We all know for instance that *cup* is a receptacle for drinking from, but if the context happens to be 'tea', I may say 'Yes, I'd like a cup' or 'She drank three cups'. Here cup has lost its normal meaning of 'receptacle' and 'a quantity of tea' has been substituted in its place. It is not the actual cup I want in this instance, but what it contains.

Metonymy is a mysterious, yet quite commonplace, interface between words and world. In its simplest form it is 'the substitution of an adjacent object'; but at its more uncanny, metonymy becomes 'the mutual penetration of objects' — metonymy in the strictest sense. Even in ordinary contexts we can observe many such instances of metonymy; so ordinary that we fail to notice them. Take the example: 'He drove six miles'. *Mile* derives ultimately from the Latin expression *milia passuum* 'a thousand paces'. Only a human being can 'walk' a thousand paces. There's no question of a mechanical object, in this instance a car, being able to do so. So, logically, *he drove six miles* will not do. But linguistically the expression is perfectly valid. The whole verbal function known as 'transivity' seems to involve metonymy. There is usually no logical connection between a (transitive) verb and its object. Take, for instance, *He heard a loud noise*. It is not 'he' that hears the loud noise, if we are to use *hear* in a strictly literal sense, but his ears. Between the ears and the representation of hearing a loud noise, there is an entire epistemology, and centuries of philosophical and aesthetic debate.

Modern poets have made wide use of metonymy and, in so doing, have made severe demands on their readers' imaginations. Here is an extract from the Russian poet, Boris Pasternak:

'The lamps only accentuated the emptiness of the evening

air...... The lamps came much less into contact with the rooms than with the spring sky which they seemed pushed up close to...' (*Safe Conduct*)

The use of the word *contact* is explicitly metonymic. Pasternak's writing teems with this kind of metonymic alchemy:

'Offshoots of rainstorm muddily clump together, and before dawn, for what a long, long time. They scrawl from rooftops their acrostics and blow their bubbles into rhyme!' (*Poetry*)

We are reminded of Shakespeare's

'Bare ruin'd choirs, where late the sweet birds sang.'

In Chinese poetry we find a mass of verbal images in contiguity, with virtually no clues from syntax as to how they are to be read. The images spill into one another, yet resist the imposition of definitive interpretations. In the poetry of the West, metre, rhythm, rhyme, assonance are, as it were, spatial and temporal projections of this very same metonymy. It is these spatial and temporal projections that render translation virtually impossible. As Pasternak himself put it: images of the surrounding world function as contiguous reflections, metonymical incarnations of the poet's self:

'Reality arises in a new kind of category. This category seems to us to be its own condition and not ours.... We try to name it. The result is art.'

European languages are so close as to be regarded as dialects of what the American linguist-anthropologist Whorf insisted on calling 'Standard Average European'. In English, for instance, we say 'It is raining', in Russian 'Rain is coming/going'; in Latin, people said 'Raineth'. Here the metonymies are similar, but doubtless there are many many languages in which even the familiar noun 'rain' is absent. In one American Indian language, for example, rain is 'water sprinkling' at the onset of a shower, and '(Water) floats with me' becomes the equivalent of 'It's raining cats and dogs'.

The metonymic process ('words hurled at things') has shaped our world in ways we do not even suspect. When we encounter language systems, 'poetic' universes, which have been separated from Eurasia by tens of thousands of years, we are in for a fair amount of 'culture shock'. The familiar noun and verb concepts with which our own world is peopled, which we take so much for granted, melt away.

In Navaho, for example, we do find verb forms; but not those familiar to us. One such is 'one animate object moves'. Such a delightfully abstruse (to us, not to the Navaho) occurs in translation equivalents of some of our most ordinary vocabulary. Compare the following:

Navaho (literal English translation)	English (idiomatic equivalent)
One moves continuously about withreference to it	'To be busy, preoccupied'
One moves into clothing	'One gets dressed'
A happening moves	'A ceremony begins'
One moves about here and there	'One lives'
One moves about newly	'Is young'
Move happenings about here and there	'Make plans'
Move words out of an enclosed space	'Sing'

And who would have supposed that in Nootka the single word-phrase that literally translates as 'Boiled eaters go for he does', means quite simply 'He invites people to a feast'?

A language, any language, may be thought of as a repository of many millennia of unrecorded metaphor and metonymy, through 'poetic' activity of one sort or another. The poet brings together the raw undifferentiated representations of our physical surroundings. As Whorf put it,

'A fair realisation of the incredible degree of diversity of linguistic system that ranges over the globe leaves one with an inescapable feeling that the human spirit is inconceivably old; that the few thousand years of history covered by our written records are no more than the thickness of a pencil mark on the scale that measures our past experience on this planet; that the events of these recent millenniums spell nothing in any evolutionary wise, that the human race has taken no sudden spurt ... but has only played a little with a few of the linguistic formulations and views of nature bequeathed from an inexpressibly longer past'.

Notes and Suggested Further Reading

The essential companion here is Owen Barfield's seminal Poetic Diction *(2nd Edn. London, 1952).*

The references for metaphor are M. Beardsley: 'The Metaphorical Twist', *published in* Philosophy and Phenomenological Research, Vol. 22, 1962; *and Paul Ricoeur* The Rule of Metaphor, *etc. (Toronto, 1975).*

The essay by Jakobson is in D. Davie and A. Livingstone (eds.): Pasternak *(London, 1969). The Navaho extracts are from H. Hoijer's article 'Cultural Implications of some Navaho Linguistic Categories', reprinted in D. Hymes:* Language in Culture and Society *(New York, 1964). The reference for Benjamin Lee Whorf is:* Language, Thought, and Reality *(New York, 1962).*

14

STICKS AND STONES

WORDS AS REALITY

Modern times have bred the convention of distinguishing between fiction and non-fiction. Anything falling within the category 'fiction' is somehow never intended to be taken as real, and any piece of writing parading as non-fiction, or truth, subsequently unmasked as 'fiction', is liable to provoke feelings of unease, disappointment or disgust.

The reasons underlying this kind of dichotomy may be fairly complex. But I would like to suggest that a part of these reasons is that words have helped to form the web of convention that we think of as 'real life'. If someone in my household informs me that there is a baby alligator at the bottom of the garden, I will dismiss this as lying, make-believe, or other, depending on the age and character of the person who has told me, simply because in more Northern latitudes there are no alligators in the wild. If it is a small child I may reply, patronisingly, 'Oh, is there? How big is he?' If on the other hand it is an older person, given to such 'fantasies', I may accuse him or her of being tedious or, if the condition is more serious, adopt other tactics. If by chance the report later turns out to have been true, I may feel it necessary to issue apologies.

The point I am coming to is that we use words all of the time not only to make true or false statements, but also to issue threats, reprimands and apologies, to cajole and persuade, to promise, coerce, make fun, give thanks, express frustration, and to 'perform' many other kinds of 'speech act'.

Until recently, it was only the writer who needed no reminding that words are more than inert tokens, 'mere words'. Most of the rest of us had virtually forgotten that words do not just stand around like pieces of furniture, that they actually do things, are constantly at work in our world, in a limitless variety of ways.

The discovery, or should one say, the *re*discovery of this 'performative' dimension of words has to be credited to the Oxford philosopher J.L. Austin. Austin was interested mainly in verbal usages which literally achieve something or bring about states of affairs; phrases like '*I bet you...*', or '*I name this ship...*', or '*You're out*' (as spoken by an umpire in a cricket match). But the functive nature of verbs extends well beyond Austin's hardcore performatives. What is nowadays referred to as 'illocutionary force' by philosophers and linguists alike can be seen to pervade almost the whole of language.

One puzzling thing about speech acts — strictly speaking, the use of language in a performative sense — is that, although they may be closely associated with particular verbal expressions, they are not wedded to them in any permanent one-to-one relationship. 'Promising' is a good example. Promising may most directly be associated with the verb *promise*, or phrases containing the noun *promise* (as in *That's a promise*). But these are not the only ways of 'promising'. When someone (in English) says 'Yes' in answer to the question 'Will you be coming this evening?', this is just as much a promise as if the words 'Yes, I promise' had been uttered. sometimes, not even words are necessary: a nod of the head, or the slightest of gestures, as in a public auction, conveys the meaning 'I promise'. And as for the verb *promise* itself, we can easily notice that it does not always indicate a 'promise'. When someone says: 'I promise you you will get into trouble if...' the speaker is issuing a warning or a threat.

The more we think about it, and well beyond its strictly performative role, the more we will notice that real language —

109

as opposed to textbook or other forms of stereotyped language — embodies an 'illocutionary force' in almost everything we say or write. If what we say tends to be devoid of this force we go down as being facetious, or just plain dull, or glib. Much of our language education, especially in our mother tongue, is devoted to the mastery of illocutionary force and speech genres. Only age brings the fullest degree of prudence and finesse. Blabmouths, smooth talkers, perpetrators of shaggy dog stories, all gather a stigma in some degree. By the time we reach mature years, most of us have developed considerable skill in exercising speech (and writing) solidarity with, and control over, our fellows. We know when to be bland, when to be cutting, when to keep silent, when to be ingratiating, and when to be downright rude.

We are not dealing with some mysterious property adhering to words or language as such. Illocutionary force is a function of social convention; it is not restricted to particular languages or speech communities, and some types of speech act may be universal. It is very difficult, for example, to imagine a language in which it is impossible to make a bet. Just as I cannot deny I made a bet in my own language, if witnesses were present, I cannot deny that I have made a bet in a foreign language (provided I did succeed in making a bet) on the grounds that I did not know the language well enough.

As soon as I successfully perform a speech act to which there adheres, by social convention, a particular kind and degree of illocutionary force, I at the same time declare my own sincerity. Whenever I make a statement, I must at the same time declare an attitude or belief in that statement even though it may be intended as ironic, or insincere, or jocular. Irony and joking are superimposed speech acts which carry different force, and which, if properly conveyed, modify what J.R. Searle has called the 'sincerity condition'. Only small children can, with impunity, ask for another ice-cream, when they don't really want one.

But although, as we have seen, illocutionary force is not inherent in particular linguistic expressions, but contingent only, we have to admit that particular speech acts embodied in particular expressions can become fixed and can stay in the language for a very long time, sometimes for centuries. These expressions must in some cases have been remembered as particularly significant, though others must have stayed in use by chance. The former are more likely to have occurred in literature or in the theatre. Many such expressions have become an everyday integral part of our language, to such an extent that we may not even know that we are quoting: from someone in history, from the Bible, from Shakespeare. What sort of illocutionary force are we unleashing when we use them to powerful effect? Or — another way of looking at the same phenomenon — could it not be that the same thing happens every time we select our words, particular words, and use them forcefully and exactly: resurrecting the dead to create the new?

You may be thinking: some of all this may well be true, but what about ordinary everyday situations where some individuals seem to manage very well without all this flummery of illocutionary force? Surely, the difference between Mr. X, who can sell any number of encyclopaedias, and myself, who could never sell any, has little or nothing to do with how skilled I am at using language.

Unfortunately, if the pundits are right, it has almost everything to do with your skill in using language. Of course, one cannot overlook factors like general appearance and charm but, once these are substracted, everything else depends quite literally on what is said (or not said) and the way and context in which one says it.

The field of investigation which covers this range of skill is nowadays called the ethnography of speaking.

You have not only to know *what* to say; that is sometimes the least important thing. But you have to know *when* to say something, *how* to say it. Though speaking, in this ethnographical sense, must be rule-governed, the variables are so many that the skill required in a particular situation may be as daunting as the learning of a new language. Much complexity is covered by the innocent phrase 'social skills'. But evidently people do begin to acquire these at an early age. Those who acquire them inadequately become the equivalent of the handicapped. You may have consummate rhetorical skill, but you may encounter difficulty in getting yourself out of a scrape. You may have the sincerest, most articulate and forceful conviction about the value of some campaign

111

you are organising or some institution you have founded, and yet may not have been able to achieve one dollar's worth of fund-raising.

Even the 'channel' is important. Have you ever been in the situation of having had to ask yourself: Shall I telephone? Shall I write? Or would a call from some third party help? Should I be casual or more formal? And so forth. The point I am wanting to make is that when a person selects a message or a channel, he or she does so from a range of alternatives which he (or she) may or may not have the requisite skill to make appropriate selections from. For bilinguals, 'channel' includes the choice of which language to use in a given situation. In Hong Kong, for example, if you are Chinese, you will use English in dealing with official bodies, like government departments, the Law Courts, or the public utilities, and so forth. But if you want to negotiate a bargain purchase you will get better results by using Cantonese.

A more strange and complex twin of the speech act is what we might for convenience call the 'literary act'.

Writing, as we have seen, cannot be dismissed as merely a secondary version of speech. If Derrida is right, then writing is somehow even prior to speech. Clearly, the written word has many advantages that the spoken word lacks. It occupies space as well as time and, not being confined to the fleeting instant, can exploit without limit the word's power to forge endless links, of form and sense, with other words, and well beyond the limits of the immediate context. One has only to think of Joyce's *Finnegan's Wake*, which exhausts the farthest possibilities of language in these respects.

Like painting and line drawing, the written word also has the power of portrayal. But, because words are enmeshed in an invisible web of sense, they can in turn conjure up other words of many diverse sorts; some of them familiar, sometimes to the point of seeming more real than real; others remote, and opaquely hard to place; some austere as oracles; others scintillating, what Nabokov called (in a reference to the style of Pushkin) 'tomfooleries of language'. Literary conceit is ancient, underpinning all writing, even the most transparent. The language of literature is so different from ordinary language that, as John Preston has said, it can be thought of as a language that is not our own, a 'second' language.

Was it not Flaubert who wilted at the thought that he, a creature of flesh and blood, would one day die, only to be survived, perhaps eternally, by his own Emma Bovary, a creature of the book, a mere phantasm of the pen? How could a fiction outlive its inventor? Yet Emma would, and did.

Melville's *Moby Dick* begins with a simple invitation - 'Call me Ishmael'. But *who* is Ishmael? Even before we read on, we are deep in story, and the words are already ringing with the vastness of the book that is to unfold. We can find Ishmael in the Bible; so we cannot treat him as pure fiction. Even if we miss the biblical allusion, Ishmael has from the outset taken on a kind of reality. He can refer to himself as 'I', just as plausibly as flesh and blood people like ourselves. to insist that it is only the reader, with his almost inbred capacity for reading books like *Moby Dick* (that capacity is real, whereas Ishmael is a fiction) does not get us round the difficulty. The 'I', the 'ego' of language, is simply a verbal role performed in a particular and unique speech situation. The problem of stabilising a constant 'unshifted' referent for Ishmael is exactly the same as for anyone else, 'real' or 'fictitious'. Is Ishmael, for instance, who bids his reader call him thus, the *same* Ishmael who at various points in the novel recedes into the background of the narrative, and at another time surfaces with his 'lectures on the anatomy of the Cetacea'? If he is the same, then who is it in the hundred-and-first chapter who addresses Ishmael? Have we to suppose that it is none other than Ishmael himself?

One of the main differences between actual speech and literary fiction, between speech act and literary act, is that the latter is not bounded by the same restrictions of space and time. A literary act is also 'issued' by an author, who can up to a point control the universe of his work. But we would no doubt be mistaken in ascribing too much importance to this difference, because even as solid three-dimensional people we are no less 'written' by the social context in which we live. Our field of possible action is dictated in some degree by the 'authorship' of our immediate environment and wider culture. The 'I' of 'I take you at your word' and the 'I' of someone officiating at a marriage ceremony, who says: 'I pronounce you man and wife', even though they may be issued by the same concrete individual, will not be the same 'I's. And both of these 'I's are different again from the 'I bequeath' as it might appear in a will read after that same person's death. Even if this 'same' individual were an author, we could not be really sure that he was the same person who once appeared in one of his stories beginning: 'One winter morning I was driving in the direction of X, when ...' It may not after all be that easy, in a domain of words, to draw a very sharp line between fiction and reality. and we may have to appeal to other dimensions, like commonsense or intuition, or rely on the blind man's stick of science.

Notes and Suggested Further Reading

Austin's major views are to be found in How to do Things with Words *(Oxford, 1962). J.R. Searle's most succinct and provocative article is 'A Classification of Illocutionary Acts', published in* Language and Society, *Volume 5, 1976.*

There is also an article by Searle ('What is a Speech Act?') in P.P. Giglioli: Language and Social Context *(Harmondsworth, 1972) which contains also a whole cluster of relevant articles, including Dell Hymes's 'Towards Ethnographies of Communication: the Analysis of Communicative Events'; K.H. Basso: 'To give up on words: silence in Western Apache Culure'; C.O. Frake: 'How to Ask for a Drink in Subanun'.*

The reader will find Hymes (ed.): Language in Culture and Society *(New York, 1964) full of interest. See also Muriel Saville-Troike* The Ethnography of Communication *(Oxford, 1982). The reference for John Preston is 'A Language not our own: The Languages of Literature' (Inaugural kecture),* Supplement to the Gazette *(University of Hong Kong), 1985.*

15

AFTERWORD

The previous pages have presented a kind of guided tour of the word. There are aspects of the word that have not been touched on at all, either because some of these aspects would have been too technical, or simply because it was not possible to include everything.

My main aim was to demonstrate that words take us into practically every sphere of our lives. They cannot safely be left to the specialist, like differential equations, or quantum mechanics. Words are a direct reflection of our own selves, our unadopted offspring. They lie in wait for us, without malice, at every turn. We only get into difficulties when we become slaves to them, or when we ignore them.

It is my hope that some of the follow-up suggestions for further reading will open up still further vistas, which have only been hinted at in these pages, or may lead the reader into further reflection.

I have deliberately not tried to underline any firm conclusions, since I do not believe that firm conclusions are possible. One may manage to reach some useful provisional kind of conclusion, but there are always other paths beckoning. This is because the behaviour of words, their manifestations, are at least as complicated as our social and interpersonal relationships on the one hand, and our personalities and nervous systems on the other.

Words are not plain black-and-white; they are coloured. Their resonances and auras carry us back into our personal pasts, as well as into the past of our own species. We are born into a network of sounds and meanings, which are not merely a flat one-dimensional contemporaneous structure, but a living tissue of everything human beings have ever been. The paths to what will become the future have already had their starting points in the midst of this tissue.

One view of the word we have been moving away from is that of an isolable formative, a mere 'substitution counter'; and a view that we have been moving towards is that of the word as a complex, many-dimensional piece of human ecology, an unisolable fragment of our human landscape. One difference between a human and a physical landscape is that the former is not only constantly shifting but utterly protean, which means that words can change, dissolve, interchange with and be substituted by other words, not easily or gratuitously, but according to principles we do not always understand.